Recent Research in Psychology

Jason S. Lee

Abstraction and Aging

A Social Psychological Analysis

Springer-Verlag
New York Berlin Heidelberg London
Paris Tokyo Hong Kong Barcelona

Jason S. Lee, Ph.D.
Department of Sociology
University of Cincinnati
Cincinnati, Ohio 45221-0378
Presently at Laboratory for Socio-economic Studies
National Institute of Mental Health
Bethesda, MD 20892

Cover: A conceptual diagram of the relationship between abstraction and concrete and stereotype thinking.

Library of Congress Cataloging-in-Publication Data
Lee, Jason S. (Jason Sandford)
Abstraction and aging / Jason S. Lee.
p. cm. — (Recent research in psychology)
Includes bibliographical references.
1. Abstraction—Age factors. I. Title. II. Series.
BF443.L44 1990 90-10279
153.2′4—dc20 CIP

Printed on acid-free paper.

Camera-ready copy provided by the author.
Printed and bound by Edward Brothers, Inc., Ann Arbor, Michigan
Printed in the United States of America.

9 8 7 6 5 4 3 2 1

ISBN 0-387-97433-4 Springer-Verlag New York Berlin Heidelberg
ISBN 3-540-97433-4 Springer-Verlag Berlin Heidelberg New York

Acknowledgements

Professor Emeritus Werner S. Landecker introduced me to abstraction from a sociological perspective about six years ago when I was a graduate student at the University of Michigan. His written work and our countless discussions on this topic guide the present volume in important ways. He originated the conception of abstraction as recognizing not just similarities but differences as well, thereby laying the foundation for distinguishing abstraction from stereotyping while seeing both as rooted in basic categorization processes. Drawing from the work of Mannheim and Simmel, he gave form and substance to the structural overlap hypothesis (chapter 4). As Principal Investigator of the 1980 Detroit Area Study, he played a central role in collecting the data that are analyzed in this study. In addition to these contributions, Werner unselfishly dedicated himself, with the scholarly passion and keen mind for which he is known, to guiding me through the dissertation on which this book is based.

The other members of my dissertation committee—Duane Alwin, Philip Converse, Elizabeth Douvan, and James House—also contributed to this work in its early stages. In 1989 the Section on Aging of the American Sociological Association recognized my dissertation with its Dissertation Award. I am grateful to the members of the Section and would like to thank David Ekerdt and Matilda Riley in particular.

A postdoctoral fellowship with the Longitudinal Study of American Youth (NSF grant SRS-8807409) of the Social Science Research Institute, Northern Illinois University, allowed me to focus on the cognitive and educational aspects of abstraction and gave me time to write this book. During this fellowship, Thomas Hoffer and Robert Suchner made especially helpful suggestions. Ann Hildreath, Laura Laughlin, Jon Miller, and Arthur Reynolds also helped in various ways.

A number of people read parts of this book at various stages in its development. The comments and suggestions of Carmi Schooler and Melvin Kohn have been of particular importance. I greatly appreciate the interest they have shown in this work. Suzanne Day, M. Clay Lewis, and Jamie Saville contributed editorial and research skills. Finally, it has been a pleasure to work with the staff at Springer-Verlag.

On a personal note, I would like to recognize those people whose concern, interest, and confidence helped make this project not just possible but worthwhile and enjoyable: Duane Alwin, Werner and Marjory Landecker, David and Trisha Lee, Mark and Wanda Lee, Carmi Schooler, John Stolte, Nadwa Rafeh, Suzanne Day, and most of all, my mother, Beulah Mize Lee.

Foreword

Whereas the study of intellectual development has long focused on patterns of growth in childhood, interest in adult intellectual development is of more recent vintage. The burgeoning life course perspective calls into question the popular belief that aging necessarily causes intellectual decline. It focuses on differential developmental patterns, asking why intellectual functioning increases for some, decreases for others, and remains stable for still others. In so doing, it reinvigorates thinking about the classic issue of what is intelligence and it calls for serious consideration of the social bases of intellectual functioning throughout life.

The study of intellectual development over the life course requires an integration of psychological and sociological orientations. Although each discipline has its own social psychology, it is generally recognized that they are insulated from one another (eg., see House, 1977). This insularity notwithstanding, the need to build bridges between the two orientations continues. For example, Riley (1989, p. xv) has observed that future research on social structure and intellectual functioning faces the "challenge of specifying *what* aspects of social structure relate to *what* aspects of psychological aging processes and of formulating testable hypotheses about the connecting *linkages*."

Riley's "challenge" has a direct parallel in House's (1981) interdisciplinary approach to the study of social structure and personality. House argues for explicit descriptions of the *macrosocial components* and *psychological processes* whose effects on one another operate in and through *microsocial interaction settings*. The orientation of Riley and House provides an overarching framework for examining the relationships among age, abstraction, and various social factors that facilitate or hinder abstraction over the life course. This book aims to carefully define abstraction and conceptually clarify its relations to theories of intelligence and cognitive development, psychometric tests and measures, and cognitive psychology and learning theory. It explores the significance of abstraction in education, work, and everyday life. It shows how measures of abstraction are developed from questionnaire items used in survey research. It examines the relationship between age and abstraction at the same time as it tests theory-based hypotheses relating abstraction to such social structural conditions as family environment, educational attainment, occupational complexity, experience of social diversity, frequency of social interaction, and retirement. Rationale for the expected effects of these social experiences on abstraction across the life course are discussed with reference to relevant sociological and psychological research.

The central purpose of this book is to address a number of issues that are basic to the study of aging and intellectual functioning in a balanced and interdisciplinary manner. In the first chapter, and indeed throughout, it deals with the meaning, measurement, and significance of a central component of intellectual functioning. It draws distinctions that the author has not found drawn explicitly and clearly elsewhere. In the second chapter, in the context of a discussion of the confound of age, period, and cohort effects, it considers the relative merits and faults of cross-sectional and longitudinal approaches to data collection. The third chapter considers a range of literature on the social shaping of thought. Here the aim is to bring together a range of research findings in need of synthesis. The fourth chapter explicates hypotheses, discusses measures, and reports the results of analyses of sample survey data, much of which is designed to empirically test a number of issues that arose in the first three chapters. The fifth and final chapter returns to and focuses more attention on three important issues that run throughout this book: a) the conceptualization and measurement of intellectual functioning, b) the determination of causality, and c) the representativeness and generalization of results. This chapter also summarizes the empirical results and explores directions for further research on abstraction, age, and social experience.

Contents

List of Figures and Tables

To Werner S. Landecher,
teacher and friend,
and to my father,
the late Paul L. Lee.

1
What is Abstraction? How is it Used? Why is it Important?

Definition. *The novel's meditative texture is supported by the armature of a few abstract terms. If I hope to avoid falling into the slough where everyone thinks he understands everything without understanding anything, not only must I select those terms with utter precision, but I must define and redefine them. A novel is often, it seems to me, nothing but a long quest for some elusive definitions.*

–Milan Kundera

When we define a word we are merely inviting others to use it as we would like it to be used.

The proper result of a good definition is to transform argument over terms into disagreements about facts, and thus open arguments to further inquiry.

–C. Wright Mills

1.1. Introduction

Like the novelist Kundera (1988) describes, the scholar must select and define central terms with care and precision. As Robert Merton (1967, pp. 143–146) says, "[t]he specification and clarification of key concepts is an indispensable phase of theoretic work," not just for reasons of theory but also in order "to institute observable indices of the social data with which empirical research is concerned." Even so, as Mills (1959, p. 34) points out, definitions are more *definite* than they are *definitive*. This first chapter, then, may be seen as a long quest for a definition of abstraction. It considers various meanings of the term and points out some important distinctions and contrasts; it reviews theoretical, psychometric, and cognitive approaches to abstraction from the literature of psychology; it provides examples of abstraction that show it to be a common rather than an esoteric mode of thought; it examines the relevance of abstraction to topics of educational importance, such as the value of higher order thinking, the teaching of such skills, and the issue of cognitive transfer; and finally, it refines the definition of abstraction by relating it to its twin opposites—concrete thinking and stereotype thinking—within a conceptual framework of generalization processes.

1.2. Definitions, Distinctions, and Contrasts

There is a wide range of meanings attributed to the word abstraction and to its grammatical variants (abstract, abstractly, abstracted). Some of these derive from its literal or etymological meaning, others from its relational or comparative meaning. The word abstraction is also sometimes used interchangeably with "abstract thinking" and "abstractness." Precise distinctions have rarely, if ever, been drawn among these various usages. This section attempts to do just that.

1.2.1. Literal Abstraction

The word *abstraction* is the nominal form of "to abstract," which comes from the Latin *abstractus,* past participle of *abstrahere. Ab-* means "away" and *trahere* means "to draw." Thus, "to abstract" literally means to draw away from, to separate, or to pull out. A somewhat more explicit literal definition of abstraction is: the cognitive process of drawing away and mentally representing an attribute (e.g., the whiteness of snow), a human quality (e.g., the honesty of an individual), or a property (e.g., the triangularity of an ancient pyramid) from the object in which it inheres. Defined as such, abstraction is a basic cognitive mechanism that is common to all but the most immediate and rudimentary modes of thought.

Usually when people use the word abstraction, or one of its grammatical variants, they have in mind some aspect of this literal meaning. Thus, for example, when it is said that certain ideas are abstract, what is meant is that they concern things that are removed from any concrete or specific application. Similarly, art is abstract when it has little or no reference to the appearance of things in nature. Even people are said to be abstracted when they are preoccupied, removed, or somehow drawn away in their thoughts from the here and now. These common usages suggest why abstraction is sometimes disparaged, as in the phrases "mere abstractions," "arid abstractions," "empty, meaningless, and out-of-touch-with-reality abstractions." Likewise, denotations of abstraction as impractical, ideal, abstruse, and difficult to understand largely derive from (but are not necessary to) the literal meaning of the term.

1.2.2. Relational Abstraction

The *relational* definition of abstraction goes beyond its literal meaning to include comparison processes. For example, Luria (1976, p. 76) defines abstraction as "comparing two objects and determining a resemblance between them." A definition of abstraction from an early edition of *Encyclopaedia Britannica* (1911, p. 77) is both relational and social psychological: "When the mind, beginning with isolated individuals, groups them together in virtue of perceived resemblances and arrives at a unity in plurality." More recently, this was generalized to: "The mental process of isolating a common element or explicating a relationship possessed by a number of things" *(Encyclopaedia Britannica,* 1983, p. 35).

In short, whereas the literal meaning of abstraction is to draw away and mentally represent a feature from the object in which it inheres, relational abstraction is the comparison of features thus abstracted and the discernment of similarities among them. This distinction is neither commonly recognized nor merely academic. The more recent *Britannica* definition cited above shows how this distinction can be glossed over. This is unfortunate because the failure to recognize the distinction between literal and relational abstraction contributes to the confusion that arises in many discussions of "abstract thinking."

In the conceptual framework developed here, *abstract thinking* is a highly inclusive category. It stands in contrast to *concrete thinking,* which is typically defined as attending only to immediately perceived objects and focusing only on their differences. It follows, then, that all modes of thought that are not concrete are abstract. Clearly, relational abstraction—defined as the detection of commonalities among distinct objects of perception—is but one member of a large set of abstract mental operations. It is important to emphasize that abstraction, literal or relational, is not synonymous with abstract thinking. Indeed, it would seem that the concept of abstract thinking is so general a notion that it should be used cautiously because it is likely to suggest so many things to so many people that it ends up signifying next to nothing, or what can be worse, signifying different things under a single rubric.

1.2.3. Abstraction Versus Abstractness

Another point of clarification concerns the distinction between *abstraction,* which is a mode of thinking, and *abstractness,* which is a characteristic of the subject matter thought about. We have seen that relational abstraction is the cognitive process of drawing away a feature of an object and relating it to another such drawn away feature using similarity-based criteria. Abstractness is an altogether distinct idea, the meaning of which is closely related to the concept of "thingness." As Bourne (1966, p. 62) explains:

> It seems clear that the concepts one deals with in everyday life differ in their abstractness. Some concepts, such as 'barn,' are relatively concrete and are based on perceptual or 'thing-like' attributes. Others, such as 'democracy,' are more general and abstract, lacking easily perceptible features and/or empirical referents.

This distinction points to another source of confusion surrounding the abstract thinking concept: sometimes it refers to the *abstractness of content* and sometimes to *nonconcrete modes of thought.*

The distinction between content and processes of thought is also useful for pointing out that abstraction can be exercised at different levels of abstractness. For example, seeing that a wheel barrel and an automobile are alike in that both are used for transporting things is an abstraction at a relatively low level of abstractness. On the other hand, an abstraction at a high level of generality is the identification of "constrained chaos" in a dripping water faucet, weather patterns across several days, and the electrical activity of normal brain functioning.

Whereas these two examples differ with regard to the abstractness of their subject matter, each is an example of abstraction—the second no more than the first.

The definitions and distinctions introduced in this section will be further clarified and extended in the pages to come. The intention thus far has been to avoid the problem described by Merton (1967, p. 74), who writes: "Too often, a single term has been used to symbolize different concepts, just as the same concept has been symbolized by different terms. Clarity of analysis and adequacy of communication are both victims of this frivolous use of words."

1.3. Psychological Perspectives on Abstraction

Abstraction has been a topic of psychological study since the early years of the discipline (Pikas, 1966). This section examines the concept as it relates to three general areas of psychology. First it takes a broad view by considering the role of abstraction in theories of human intelligence, then it takes an applied view by examining how abstraction is conceived of and measured in psychometrics and testing, and finally it takes a microscopic view by relating abstraction to theories of cognitive psychology.

1.3.1. A Short History of Theories of Intelligence: A Broad View

The cognitive process of abstraction can be identified in all but the earliest of the best known modern theories of human intelligence. In the late 19th century, Sir Frances Galton and James Cattell conducted experiments involving the measurement of sensory discriminative capacity, reaction time, sensitivity to pain, and memory. They were primarily concerned with the sensorimotoric bases of intelligence, as reflected by the fact that they dealt with relatively simple intellectual functions and reactions that are heavily dependent on biological factors (Graham & Lilly, 1984). Abstraction has little relevance to their experiments or to their conception of intelligence. It was not long, however, before abstraction found its way into the first standardized intelligence test, published in 1905 by Alfred Binet and Theodore Simon. This was a diversified battery of subtests with an emphasis on the "higher" mental processes (Brody & Brody, 1976). Abstraction is involved in the subtest that requires "finding the similarity between two things." A related task is found in the Verbal Relations Subtest of the widely used Stanford-Binet Intelligence Scale of today. The following item illustrates the questions on this subtest.

Tell how the first three things are alike but different from the fourth:

coffee, tea, apple juice NOT cake

Since the turn of the century there has been a great deal of debate as to whether tests of particular intellectual functions should be combined into a single index or whether they should be kept separate. Karl Spearman's solution, his two-factor theory of intelligence, requires that each side concede the validity of the other without giving up its own position. Spearman believed that all tests and measures of intelligence share a common component, which he called *g* for *general,* and a unique component, which he called *s* for *specific*. According to Brody and Brody (1976, p. 11), "Spearman came to the view that *g* was principally related to the ability to perform intellectual operations he called 'eduction of relations and correlates'." Now it is interesting to note that eduction and abstraction have precisely the same literal definitions: "to call forth; to bring out," which suggests a central role for literal abstraction, at least, in Spearman's conception of *g*. But in addition, the relevance of relational abstraction to *g* is suggested in Spearman's own description of the eduction of relations as

> when a person has in mind any two or more ideas (using this word to embrace any items of mental content . . .) he has more or less power to bring to mind any relations that essentially hold between them [quoted in Brody & Brody, 1976, p. 11].

Still other descriptions of Spearman's *g,* such as "the eduction of relations among abstract items" (Anastasi, 1982), suggest an intellectual orientation as broad and indiscriminate as the concept of abstract thinking, which we have already had cause to consider critically.

In contrast to Spearman's efforts to identify a single common factor in all intelligence tests, Thurstone searched for a "simple structure" of primary mental abilities. In 1938 he published the results of a factor analysis, in which he identified 11 factors, from a battery of 56 tests administered to about 200 college students. Since that time the number has been pared down to five major abilities: verbal meaning, reasoning, space, number, and word fluency (Schaie, 1983, p. 64). According to Schaie, Thurstone "proposed that persons with good reasoning ability could solve problems, foresee consequences, analyze a situation on the basis of past experience, and make and carry out plans according to recognized facts" (p. 73). A typical item used to measure reasoning ability requires the detection of a relationship that several items have in common in order to complete a series. The following is an example:

> Choose one item from the list on the right that best completes the series on the left:
>
> a b x c d x e f x g h x   h i j k x y

This exercise requires abstraction to discern the pattern on the left (single x's between consecutive pairs of letters of the alphabet) which leads to selecting the letter on the right (i) that fits this pattern.

In more recent years Horn and Donaldson (1976) have proposed a "theory of two major forms of intelligence," which draws on Raymond Cattell's (1963) characterization of *crystallized* and *fluid* intellectual abilities. It is said that crystallized abilities are acquired through experience and are improved by "the increased learning, the consolidation of knowledge in improved concepts, the extended application of problem solving-techniques, and the increased opportunities for facilitation and positive transfer which *(ex hypothesi)* accompany aging" (Horn & Donaldson, 1976, p. 706). Fluid intelligence, on the other hand, is described as "innate general cognitive capacity—and is measured by tests that call for productive relational thinking and mental speed, but require no special knowledge or experience" (Bromley, 1974, p. 202). Moreover, fluid intellectual abilities are said to be sensitive to "negative transfer and related 'rigidities' produced by accumulated learning, and any loss or degeneration of the physiological (principally neurological) substratum supporting intellectual behavior" (Horn & Donaldson, 1976, p. 706). Finally, in a statement that reveals a degree of overlap between the types, it is said that fluid intelligence is "reflected in tests of figural relations, memory span, induction, and most processes involved in acquiring new information" (Salthouse, 1982, p. 69).

In this conceptual framework, abstraction is not clearly more one or the other type of intellectual ability. It has already been shown that abstraction is pertinent to relational thinking (a fluid ability) and it will be shown in a later section of this chapter that abstraction is central to concept formation and induction (crystallized abilities). The predicament, if you will, of not knowing which domain abstraction falls into arises from the oversimplification of "the consolidation of knowledge in improved concepts" as the product of experience, and of induction and relational thinking as biologically based cognitive capacities that are largely independent of specific knowledge or experience.

The oversimplification of intellectual functioning, as expressed in efforts to develop an overarching typologies, is part and parcel of the fallacy of reifying human intelligence (Gould, 1981). Intelligence is reified by conceiving of it unidimensionally, as in the concepts of "IQ" and "higher order thinking," or dichotomously, as in such global contrasts as fluid versus crystallized intelligence, concrete versus abstract thinking, and subject specific versus heuristic knowledge. While this is not to say that these concepts are useless, it does stress that they are easily misunderstood and prone to misuse. This suggests part of the rationale for focusing on a specific mode of thought such as abstraction. It can be carefully defined and related to other areas of psychological and sociological interest without the assumption that one has hit upon the overarching framework to explain all of human intellectual functioning.[1]

1.3.2. Psychometrics: An Applied View

A systematic review of the *Mental Measurements Yearbooks* and *Tests in Print* (Buros, 1938–1985) reveals four basic types of tests used to measure abstraction:

---

[1]Much contemporary work on intelligence has been greatly influenced by cognitive science and information processing research and avoids the reification fallacy by focusing on multiple dimensions of intelligence (e.g., Gardner's [1983] multiple intelligences), by interrelating a number of intellectual components into a hierarchy of functions (e.g., Sternberg's [1985] triarchic theory of intelligence), or by focusing on relatively specific modes of thought. For examples of the latter see Holland, Holyoak, Nisbett, and Thagard (1986) on induction; a volume edited by Rosch and Lloyd (1978) on categorization; Sternberg (1977) and Holyoak (1984) on analogical reasoning; Newell and Simon (1972) on problem solving; Nisbett and Ross (1980) on inference.

TABLE 1.1. A compendium of abstraction and abstraction-related tests

Clinical	Educational	Others
Shipley–Institute of Living Scale for Measuring Intellectual Impairment[2] (1939/1982)	Miller Analogies Test[2] (1926/1975)	Similarites Subtest of the Wechsler Adult Intelligence Scale–Revised[6] (1981)
Goldstein–Scheerer Tests of Abstract and Concrete Thinking[1] (1941/1951)	Raven's Progressive Matrices[4/2] (1938/1983)	Verbal Relations Subtest of the Stanford–Binet Intelligence Scale[8] (1986)
Gorham's Proverbs Test[3] (1956)	Croft Readiness Assessment in Comprehension Kit[5] (1978)	Abstract Reasoning Subtest of the Differential Aptitude Test (1947/1983)
Wisconsin Card Sorting Test[1] (1980)	Otis–Lennon School Ability Test[8] (1979/1982)	Cattell's Culture Fair Intelligence Test[7] (1949/1957)

[1]Sort objects according to a principle of class membership.
[2]Grasp the relationship involved in a progressive series of items and complete the final missing member of the series.
[3]Change the concrete symbols of proverbs into generalized concepts.
[4]Eduction of relations among abstract items.
[5]Measures comprehension in terms of three "levels of proficiency": concrete, semiabstract and abstract. Contrary to appearances, however, abstraction is not involved in this test.
[6]Examinees are given 14 pairs of words and must indicate in what way they are alike. A sample question is 'In what way are a ring and a necklace alike?.'
[7]The tests have no verbal content and require examinees to perceive relationships in shapes and figures.
[8]One must see what 3 or 4 things have in common and how they differ from one other thing, or, one must see what 3 things have in common and select a fourth thing that shares membership in this category from a list of alternatives.

completing letter, word, or picture series; making verbal analogies of the form "*a* is to *b* as *c* is to ____?"; translating proverbs into generalized ideas; and sorting objects. For present purposes, however, the specific tests identified in this review are classified according to their design and use. First we consider measures of abstraction used by clinicians, primarily in psychiatric contexts, then we consider measures of abstraction used for educational evaluation, screening, and placement, and finally we consider a residual category of abstraction-related tests used for such purposes as occupational counseling and the measurement of general intelligence. It will become apparent that the conceptualization of abstraction varies both within and between these areas and that the conceptual distinctions drawn earlier are useful for sorting out which tests are relevant for our purposes and which are not. As a guide through this review, a compendium of the tests discussed here is presented in Table 1.1.

1.3.2.1. PSYCHIATRIC/CLINICAL USES

The most common use of tests explicitly designed to measure abstraction is the identification of intellectual impairment. One of the earliest, if not the earliest, such test is the Shipley-Institute of Living Scale for Measuring Intellectual

Impairment, which was first published in 1939 (and was revised as recently as 1982). A reviewer writes that "abstract reasoning is measured by a 20-item abstraction test in which the subject is asked to grasp the relationship involved in a progressive series of items and complete the final missing member of the series" (Hunt, 1949, p. 195). Another reviewer explains that the concern with abstraction derives from the belief that conceptual ability declines more quickly than vocabulary ability in cases of intellectual decrement (Ives, 1949). Clearly, abstraction is seen as basic to the formation of concepts.

The Goldstein-Scheerer Tests of Abstract and Concrete Thinking, originally published in 1941 and last revised 10 years later, were designed by two physicians who worked with brain-damaged patients during and following World War I (Goldstein, 1963; Payne, 1965). Abstraction is measured by having the testee sort objects (blocks, sticks, skeins, and geometric shapes) according to various and sometimes changing criteria. Goldstein and Scheerer (1941) believe that the main effect of brain damage on thinking is impairment of the "abstract attitude," which results in over-reliance on concrete phenomena. The abstract and concrete attitudes, they write, are not "acquired mental sets or habits of the individual, or special isolable aptitudes. They are rather *capacity levels of the total personality.*" The concrete attitude is "confined to immediate apprehension of a given thing or situation in its particular uniqueness" (pp. 2–3; compare with the definition of concrete thinking suggested above). Furthermore, they argue, it is characterized by rigidity and the "'lack of shifting' well known in abnormal psychology. The concrete attitude exists also in respect to ideas, thoughts, and feelings" (p. 3). On the other hand, they continue, the abstract attitude

> implies conscious activity in the sense of reasoning, awareness and self-account of one's doing. We transcend the immediately given situation, the specific aspect or sense impression; we abstract common from particular properties; we are oriented in our action by a rather conceptual viewpoint, be it a category, a class, or a general meaning under which the particular object before us falls" [pp. 3–4].

It is apparent that Goldstein and Scheerer tend to conceive of abstraction more along the lines of abstract thinking in general, rather than in its specific relational sense.

Gorham's (1956) Proverbs Test is another measure of intellectual impairment designed to assess the "abstracting function" or "levels of concrete and abstract reasoning" (Martin, 1967, p. 594). It was first published in 1956 as a set of three 12-item parallel forms and included such proverbs as: *Rome was not built in a day, let sleeping dogs lie,* and *a disease known is half cured.* Gorham (1956, p. 1) explains that converting the "concrete symbols of the proverbs into generalized concepts" requires abstraction. After acquiring considerable clinical experience with this test, he gave it a multiple-choice format. For example, the following are the test items for the three proverbs quoted above.

1. Rome was not built in a day.
   a) It takes some things longer to happen than others.
   b) It took a number of years.
   c) Great things come about slowly.
   d) You can't do certain things in a day.
2. Let sleeping dogs lie.
   a) Don't stir up old troubles.
   b) Be kind to dumb animals.
   c) Let those who don't wish to learn alone.
   d) Because he might bite.
3. A disease known is half cured.
   a) A good doctor can tell what is wrong with you.
   b) You have to understand the problem before you can cure it.
   c) You can only half cure some things.
   d) Diagnosis comes before treatment.

The multiple-choice format vastly simplifies coding because it eliminates the need for clinical training in order to interpret responses to open-ended questions. On the other hand, the vocabulary and reading skills required are not insignificant.[2]

The last measure of abstraction designed for clinical purposes considered here is the Wisconsin Card Sorting Test (WCST). It was first published in 1980 and is described as a "neurological instrument for diagnosing brain damage" (Egeland, 1985, p. 1746). Like the Goldstein-Scheerer battery, the WCST requires abstraction to mentally draw out shared features of objects, which in turn provides the basis for sorting the objects according to class membership. Although the purpose of this and other sorting tests is to detect intellectual impairment, we must question the validity of such judgments without knowledge about the full range of sorting skills of the intellectually unimpaired. Consider as an example that Egeland (1985) describes a study in which data were collected on the WCST from patients who were clinically referred for a neurological examination and from normal subjects. Score boundaries separating the suspected impaired from the nonimpaired were determined by selecting the point below which the majority (about 70%) of the neurology patients scored and above which about the same percentage of the normal subjects scored. Yet, as Egeland (p. 1746) observes,

> the normals who were over 59 years old and who obtained less than a 12th-grade education scored in the impaired range. The author [of the WCST manual] suggests an alternate cutoff score for older subjects but he does not provide any normative data to support whether or not this is an appropriate score. Clearly, there is a need for more adequate norms, *particularly by age and education* [emphasis added].

[2]These and related issues are examined in chapter 4 where the development of a measure of abstraction for use in survey research is discussed.

This example illustrates that we must guard against drawing conclusions about human intellectual functioning from findings based on special subgroups of subjects. Without representative samples or adequate norming data, against what standard can one compare the range of performances actually observed? There would seem to be much of interest and importance to learn about variation in intellectual functioning due to social and developmental factors.

1.3.2.2. Educational Uses

The Miller Analogies Test (MAT) is widely used in the selection of candidates for graduate school and for high-level positions in business. Originally published in 1926 and last revised in 1975, the MAT consists of 100 verbal analogy items of the form "*a* is to *b*, as *c* is to _____?" with the correct answer listed among four response options. Even though it can be argued that abstraction is used to discern the relationship between an *a* and *b* that is also shared by a *c* and one of the possible *d* responses, some reviewers (e.g., Willingham, 1965; Schrader, 1965) are skeptical about whether the MAT measures anything other than verbal ability or vocabulary knowledge. This complaint, although somewhat exaggerated, is reasonable, as most who have taken the MAT would probably agree, and it does serve to suggest that any test that uses the analogy to measure abstraction per se should avoid a heavy emphasis on vocabulary skills.[3]

Another popular test that has been around for quite some time is J.C. Raven's Progressive Matrices (PM), originally published in Britain in 1938 and revised as recently as 1983. Each of its three forms is composed of tasks requiring the completion of designs within matrices; in other words, the PM is a series completion task test. Anastasi (1982, p. 290) observes that there is agreement among most British psychologists that the PM is the best existing measure of Spearman's general component of intelligence. Given that Spearman believed "tests dealing with abstract relations are probably the best measures of '*g*' " (Anastasi, p. 366), and that the PM is considered the best measure of *g*, then the PM must be a measure of the ability to deal with abstract relations. Already we have concluded that this notion—the ability to deal with abstract relations—is synonymous with the concept of abstract thinking. Recall that the critique of this concept focuses on its overinclusiveness and indiscriminateness. It does include abstraction—both literal and relational—but then, it embraces just about any mode of thought that is not concrete and particularistic. A reviewer (Bortner, 1965, p. 764) of the PM makes a similar point and highlights the need for further research:

> [W]hat does it signify to be able to break up designs into constituent parts, to find perceptual analogies, to complete a design, etc.? In the absence of developmental data

---

[3]Luria (1976) provides some examples of items similar to those in the MAT but that are much less likely to confound verbal skill with abstraction performance. See also the analogy items in Sternberg (1986).

concerning these aspects of perceptual adequacy, and their relation to other factors in intelligence, they remain theoretical constructs.

The view taken here is that although the PM may indeed involve abstraction, it does not measure abstraction alone and that, for our purposes, this confounding of multiple modes of thought is undesirable.

A test designed for educational purposes that *appears* to involve abstraction but really has little to do with it is the Croft Readiness Assessment in Comprehension Kit, published in 1978. It is said that this test is designed to assess oral and written language comprehension and pattern recognition at concrete, semiabstract, and abstract levels of proficiency (Weinshank, 1985, p. 417). It is tempting to lump together all measures that have some variant of the word abstract in their title or description, but observe that this test is concerned with comprehension at various *levels of abstractness* (generality) rather than with the comprehension or production of abstractions. This observation reinforces the validity and significance of the distinction between *abstraction* and *abstractness.*

Test items designed for educational purposes that clearly do require the use of relational abstraction are found in the Otis-Lennon School Ability Test. Two such examples are:

1. Which word does *not* go with the other four?
   a. trail b. map c. highway d. street e. path

2. Which thing most clearly goes with: **scissors** **wire** **penny**
   a. dollar bill b. key c. string d. pencil e. paper

The first item requires abstraction to see that a trail, highway, street, and path are things you travel on, whereas a map is what you use to find your way about. The second item requires abstraction to see that scissors, wire, and a penny are made of metal and, therefore, that key is the correct response. It should be noted that because these kinds of questions deal with simple subject matter, it is reasonable to assume that people across a range of backgrounds and ages would be familiar with these topics and, thus, that what differentiates their responses is skill in using abstraction. The same cannot be said for questions that try to measure abstraction using difficult vocabulary items that require knowledge of scientific facts or mathematical symbols or that involve the reading of detailed literary passages.[4]

[4]Indeed, the vast majority of tests used to assess students' knowledge and thinking skills require a multiplicity of intellectual functions in individual items. This is needed for the evaluation of overall competence, but it provides little information about specific cognitive skills, such as abstraction. For example, in a question that requires abstraction and reading skill and knowledge of a scientific principle, who can know where the deficit lies in an incorrect answer?

1.3.2.3. Other Uses

The Abstract Reasoning Test from the Differential Aptitude Test, parts of Cattell's Culture Fair Intelligence Test, the Similarities Test from the Wechsler Adult Intelligence Scale (WAIS) and the Wechsler Intelligence Scale for Children (WISC), and the Verbal Relations Test from the Stanford–Binet Intelligence Scale also require abstraction, as do such tests of creativity as the Torrence Tests of Creative Thinking and Guilford's Tests of Divergent Thinking from the Aptitudes Research Project. Of these, probably the best measures of relational abstraction are the Similarities Test of the Wechsler batteries and the Verbal Relations Test from the Standford–Binet.

Matarazzo (1972, p. 488) observes that "the Similarities test is often designated as a test of abstraction" and that Wechsler intended that it measure "the individual's ability to perceive the common elements of the terms he is asked to compare and, at higher levels, his ability to bring them under a single concept" (p. 206). Below is a description of the test and some examples of items from various editions.

> Examinees are given 14 pairs of words and must indicate in what way they are alike. Items are scored 2, 1, or 0. Testing is discontinued after four consecutive failures. A sample question would be: "In what way are a ring and a necklace alike?" This test requires the examinee to see or discover the common elements of the terms being compared [Graham & Lilly, 1984, p. 98].

Some word pairs are:

Orange . . . . Banana
Air . . . . Water
North . . . . West
Radio . . . . Telephone
Mountain . . . . Lake
Liberty . . . . Justice

It may be recalled from the example provided earlier that Verbal Relations questions ask the examinee to state how three things are alike and how they differ from a fourth thing. Another example of these items is: "Robin, sparrow, eagle, NOT penguin." Further discussion of these tests is reserved for chapter 4, at which time their scoring criteria are examined for their relevance to the measure of abstraction used in this study.

1.3.3. Cognitive Psychology: A Microscopic View

This section suggests how abstraction is used to build up more complex knowledge structures through classification and concept formation. Readers with some exposure to cognitive psychological literature will recognize familiar concepts and theories in the framework developed below. Although some connections between this conceptual framework and other models of thinking, learning, and knowledge development are specified, more needs to be done than what is attempted here.

Some of the earliest insights to come out of the study of cognitive psychology relate to the fact that the mind is less a receptacle for, than a filter of, environmental stimuli. That is, we do not passively receive information so much as we actively process it. We selectively attend to, sharpen, and level stimuli, thereby somewhat idiosyncratically adding to and taking away from reality as we know it. A basic process in the creation of meanings is the grouping of objects of perception and relating them to one another according to various classificatory schemes. Categories thus formed henceforth influence how we see new things as well as how we come to see old things anew. Thus, an important part of learning involves the development of new categories and concepts. Abstraction is one cognitive mechanism used for this purpose because it involves the encoding and retrieval of information according to similarity and (as we see later in this chapter) difference criteria. The categories or concepts thus formed become the foundation for further knowledge, or possibly for stereotypes (also discussed in this chapter) and prejudices (discussed in chapter 3).

We can think of the development of new concepts and categories as the "building blocks" of a more complex knowledge "structure." Information is either assimilated to existing categories or used to accommodate new ones. New categories, of course, are not like islands unto themselves. They are connected with pre-existing cognitive structures according to a host of criteria. Abstraction involves linking new categories and concepts with old ones on the basis of similarities and differences. The criteria used to judge commonalities and differences vary widely; for example, some are at the level of surface qualities and appearances, whereas others are concerned with less manifest characteristics. To be more specific, similarities and differences may be observed with respect to such matters as causality, temporal association, function, purpose, form, location, and proprietorship. Any number of considerations may link ideas and concepts together in the mind. As a general rule, the more categories and the more intricate the linkages between them, the more structurally complex the knowledge system.

Imagine for a moment looking at a sample of tissue from the cerebral cortex and seeing a portion of the interconnections among the brain's 10 billion neurons across some 10^{15} synapses. That is a complex structure. This may help one visualize inter-relationships among concepts and categories in a complex knowledge structure. The parallel is not perfect. No one knows exactly how knowledge is represented in the electrical and chemical transactions across neurons. But at the very least, parsimony is achieved in using the same model to represent the neural structure of the brain and the knowledge structure of the mind.[5]

[5]This idea gains some support from Nobel laureate Gerald Edelman, who says that because "cell-to-cell connections in the brain are far too numerous and variable to be specified in detail by a person's genetic blueprint," certain combinations of connections are strengthened through response to environmental stimulation. In fact, he goes so far as to say that "every experience in a person's life alters and shapes that individual's brain" (Hellerstein, 1988). These ideas are the linchpin of the study of the social shaping of thought.

The conceptual framework just elaborated has a number of parallels in cognitive psychological literature on knowledge representation and concept formation. For example, a number of cognitive psychologists assume that *predictive* and *classificatory rules* are the most basic epistimic unit used to structure information. They conceive of these rules as clustered into hierarchical arrangements around a "default" or basic level of categorization that "allows us to reduce differences among all the objects in our environment without wiping out the important differences among objects" (Mayer, 1983, p. 249; see also Holland et al., 1986; Rosch, Mervis, Gray, Johnson, & Boyes-Braem, 1976). In the *schema* or *connectionist* model of knowledge representation the concept of rules is replaced with the concept of propositions. Accordingly, factual knowledge is viewed as comprised of networks of propositional representations stored in long-term memory and activated (brought into working memory) by various thought processes. Activation spreads simultaneously along all paths emanating from a particular locus, and both the existence and the activation potential of these connections are understood to be influenced by prior experience (see the previous footnote) (Mayer, 1983, chap. 9; Stillings et al., 1987, pp. 21-36). Similar parallels can be drawn to Rosch's (1978) "prototype" approach to categorization and to Bolton's (1977) in-depth treatment of concept formation.

In brief, abstraction is a basic cognitive process used in the formation of concepts and thus in the structuring of knowledge. The cognitive framework sketched out here provides a guideline for thinking about the development of abstraction across the life course and the role of abstraction in various aspects of life course development—topics that are taken up in later chapters.

1.4. Some Concrete Abstractions

In general terms, the significance of abstraction lies in its contribution to learning and to solving problems. When one talks about "learning from experience," what is meant is that a current problem should be understood as similar in some significant way to a problem in the past for which one already has a workable solution. The significance of this use of abstraction is expressed more generally in George Santayana's (1954) adage: "Those who cannot remember the past are condemned to repeat it."

Abstraction is not *only* used in learning and problem solving; it has numerous uses in a multitude of contexts. Abstraction is not merely an academic exercise restricted to the ivory tower, as the following examples are intended to show. Each one illustrates an abstraction, and together they signify the range of uses to which this mode of thought is put. The reader may test his or her own comprehension of the concept by summarizing in a single sentence the abstraction in each of these examples.

1. So in Washington we go on arguing about Nicaragua, and in Moscow they go on arguing about Afghanistan, and in Europe the governments argue about trade and the cost of vegetables. But somehow nobody seems ever to get around to the things they have in common . . . . One thing they have in common is that all their ideological theories and systems of politics are failing to deal with the realities of human nature [Reston, 1986].
2. But if they differ in some respects, there is still a major similarity among all the learned professions. Each of them possesses large stocks of complex and advanced knowledge which have not been mastered by the laity of clients, patients, and students to whom the learned professions address themselves [Shils, 1983, p. 9].
3. Fast times, however, are about all that [Priscilla] Welch [a 42-year-old British marathon runner] has in common with the elite company she keeps on the roads. Unlike Waitz, Joan Benoit Samuelson and Kristiansen, she is not a one-time track star or cross country runner who has found gold on city streets around the world [Alfano, 1987].

The fourth example of abstraction is from a letter to former acting Prime Minister of Italy, Bettino Craxi from former President Ronald Reagan.

4. During the last week, we have had differences on the best way to respond to the hijacking of the *Achille Lauro*. Despite these differences, which we have dealt with in a frank and friendly way, we share fundamental commitments on the necessity to respond with firmness to the threat of international terrorism [*NYT*, 1985].

The next example is an excerpt from an interview given by Theodore Bundy, a diagnosed psychopath and convicted mass murderer who was executed in Florida in 1989.

5. [F]or people to want to condemn someone, to dehumanize someone like me, is a very popular and effective way of dealing with a fear and a threat that is just incomprehensible. It's sort of like the old cliche of the ostrich sticking its head in the sand. When people go to those cliches that someone is a monster beyond help, that he's demented, that he's got some kind of defect, then they're sticking their heads in that ground of ignorance. You see, because if you think that way then there's no way you're ever going to confront the real sources of the problem. When they fail to see their common humanity with me, when they can't link up together like you and I are right now, when people are not ready to see me as I am, they propose these stereotypes [NYT, 1986].

In the final example, Hannah Arendt observes that Marx equates the relationship between labor pangs and birth to the relationship between violence and revolution.

6. The more dubious and uncertain an instrument violence has become in international relations, the more it has gained in reputation and appeal in domestic affairs, specifically in the matter of revolution. The strong Marxist rhetoric of the New Left coincides with the steady growth of the entirely non-Marxist conviction, proclaimed by Mao Tsetung, that "Power grows out of the barrel of a gun." To be sure, Marx was aware of the role of violence in history, but this role was to him secondary; not violence but the contradictions inherent in the old society brought about its end. The emergence of a new society was preceded, but not caused, by violent outbreaks, which he likened to the labor pangs that precede, but of course do not cause, the event of organic birth [Arendt, 1970, p. 11].

1.5. Abstraction in Education

Having shown that abstraction is an important part of learning and problem solving, and having indicated that it has a multitude of everyday uses, the next topic to consider is the more general relevance of abstraction to education. In later chapters we will see that education consistently stands out as a major determinant of intellectual and psychological functioning. In this section, the concept of abstraction and issues of educational relevance come together in a discussion of the concept of *higher order thinking*.

1.5.1. Higher Order Thinking in School and Beyond

The widely publicized lagging performance of U.S. students on achievement tests is considered to be due, in part, to a deficiency in higher order thinking and reasoning strategies (National Academy of Education, 1987; National Science Board Commission on Precollege Education in Mathematics, Science and Technology, 1983). Most of the tests are designed so that one must use thinking skills in combination with knowledge of facts in order to solve problems. And yet, as stated in a report from the American Association for the Advancement of Science, "schoolchildren today are being overwhelmed with specific facts and formulas but rarely see the vital relationships that link what they are learning" (Van, 1989). This conclusion is supported by data from national assessments showing that even as students' performance on calculation tasks has risen, their mathematics problem solving skills have declined (National Assessment of Educational Progress, 1983; Resnick, 1987, p. 14).

Both in schools and in the assessment of educational outcomes, increasing emphasis is being placed on the view that good teaching is not simply a matter of conveying information for students to remember. Thus, it is believed that one of the most important ways teachers can help students learn is by showing them "how to use their minds more effectively—how to think clearly, critically, and coherently" (Miller, 1986, p. 2). The importance of such skills clearly extends well beyond formal schooling. Roger Smith, chairman of General Motors, made this point with remarkable clarity and insight in a speech he delivered at the University of Michigan on the importance of a liberal arts education to business and management.

> In an environment of rapid and constant change, a company's competitiveness—and in some cases, survival itself—depends on managers with vision. We need people who can think of new strategies, as well as new ways of carrying out old ones. We need people who can extrapolate on the basis of what worked in the past, people who can organize and reorganize operations so that economy is achieved and redundancy eliminated, people who can imagine how the course of events might be changed, and by what kind of interventions . . . .
>
> These mental processes can be acquired in the study of the liberal arts. You're trained to *recognize recurring elements and common themes* in art and literature, in physics and history, so you learn to *see the relations between things that may seem utterly different and*

to combine familiar elements into new forms. You learn to *connect the seemingly unconnected.* In other words, you learn about the kind of creativity that leads to visionary solutions to business problems [Smith, 1985, p. 4, italics added to draw attention to the similarity to abstraction].

What distinguishes this statement from other statements of the value of education to life beyond school is its precision. This is not merely a sentiment about the importance of "higher order thinking," a phrase whose popularity is matched by the confusion surrounding its use. Instead it is an elaboration of a particular mode of thought (seeing relations between things that may seem utterly different) that underlies specific skills (recognizing common themes and combining familiar elements into new forms) that are used to solve business problems (specified in the first paragraph of the excerpt).

If it is possible to focus on the relevance of specific modes of thought such as abstraction to education and to life beyond school, does it follow that the concept of higher order thinking is simply a category label for this and all other such cognitive processes? The answer to this will become obvious below.

1.5.2. What is Higher Order Thinking Anyway?

The 1980s witnessed a rapid increase in research on higher order thinking (see Figure 1.1). One conclusion this literature clearly supports is that there is little agreement about what the higher order thinking concept means or what range of mental operations it encompasses. For example, Resnick (1987, p. 3) says that "[a]lthough we cannot define it exactly, we can recognize higher order thinking when it occurs": it is effortful, complex, self-regulating and nonalgorithmic; it involves uncertainty, nuanced judgment, the imposition of meaning, and the application of multiple criteria; and finally, it yields multiple solutions. Resnick demonstrates that higher order thinking is a global concept (like justice, freedom, democracy, intelligence, abstract thinking, and others) that is useful at a very general level of discourse. But she also demonstrates, implicitly and not apparently intentionally, that the concept is not suitable at a more analytic level. Table 1.2 reinforces this point by listing more than two dozen phrases and terms used as synonyms for higher order thinking compiled from only two sources that deal with the topic in detail and with authority (Resnick's [1987] monograph titled *Education and Learning to Think* and *The Nation's Report Card* from the National Academy of Education [1987]).

Like the concepts of intelligence and abstract thinking, the higher order thinking concept is easily reified. Gould (1981, p. 151) is perhaps the most eloquent critic of reification, which he describes as "the logical error that John Stuart Mill had identified—'to believe that whatever received a name must be an entity or being, having an independent existence of its own'." Maybe we should abandon the higher order thinking phrase altogether. Indeed, Marzanio and Hutchins (1985, p. 2) write that "[c]urrent research and theory on information processing or 'thinking' does not support a distinction between a set of 'lower' level skills

TABLE 1.2. A list of synonymous phrases used for "higher order thinking"

Reasoning, logical reasoning skills
Rhetoric
Mathematical and scientific thought
Critical thinking
Independent thinking
Nonroutine thinking
Monitoring one's understanding
Executive, self-regulating, metacognitive processes
Imposing meaning and structure
Elaborating, adding complexity, going beyond the given
Weighing multiple alternatives
Accepting uncertainty
Carrying out extended analysis
Solving open-ended problems
Command of complex relationships
Recognizing a problem's general structure
Defining goals
Isolating the information relevant to problem situations
Evaluating the merits of arguments
Analyzing
Explaining
Finding analogies
Skills that enable one to organize, coordinate and direct lower level skills effectively
Problem solving:
Consider multiple sides of an issue
Consider consequences
Select objectives and weigh factors involved in a situation
Generate and evaluate evidence

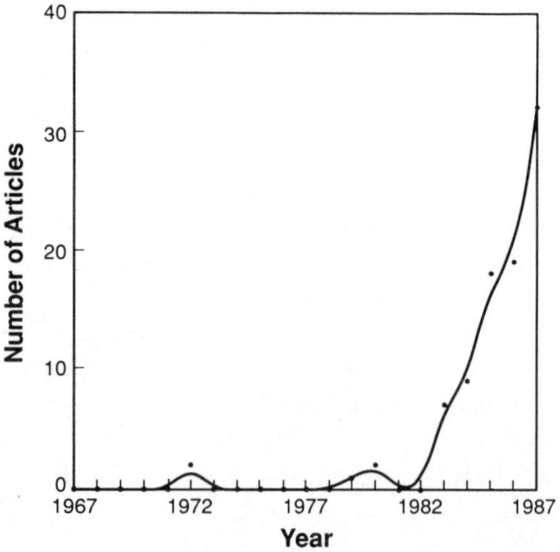

FIGURE 1.1. Trend in Research on Higher Order Thinking: 1967-1987

and a different set of 'higher' skills." They submit that a more valid higher/lower distinction concerns the indwelling levels of complexity of the content we master and problems we solve. (Here is further evidence of the significance of the distinction between processes and content of thought and between abstraction and abstractness.)

Although Resnick (1987, p. 3) believes that "we can recognize higher order thinking when it occurs," she does acknowledge that "[t]he term 'higher order' skills is probably itself fundamentally misleading, for it suggests that another set of skills, presumably called 'lower order' need to come first." Yet, she explains,

> [t]he most important single message of modern research on the nature of thinking is that the kinds of activities traditionally associated with thinking are not limited to advanced levels of development. Instead, these activities are an intimate part of even elementary levels of reading, mathematics, and other branches of learning—when learning is proceeding well [p. 8].

This statement takes on added relevance in chapter 2 when the role of abstraction in early cognitive development is discussed.

1.5.3. Teaching Abstraction

The excerpt from Roger Smith's speech provides an excellent initial statement of how schools provide instruction in abstraction. He says that in the study of the liberal arts "you're trained to recognize recurring elements and common themes in art and literature, in physics and history, so you learn to see the relations between things that may seem utterly different and to combine familiar elements into new forms." Although he focuses specifically on higher education, training of this kind begins with the first lesson in *comparing and contrasting* things. Finding similarities and differences, stating how two or more things are alike and how they are distinct, comparing and contrasting—however it is said—abstraction is exercised at all levels of educational curricula.

Abstraction is not taught only in one or a few disciplines or areas, but is common to all subjects. Perhaps because abstraction is both elementary and ubiquitous, teachers are not likely to be aware that they are teaching it. Abstraction is exercised in the study of history when students compare and contrast events preceding wars as they look for common and unique causes, when they look for similarities and differences in the reigns of succeeding monarchs, and when they search for commonalities across the seemingly different revolutions in America, France, and Russia. Abstraction is exercised in the study of literature whenever students look for common and unique themes across literary periods and when they compare and contrast writing styles and techniques.

The use of abstraction is no less obvious in science and mathematics. The Educational Testing Service's National Assessment of Educational Progress (1986a, p. 13) describes a "key mathematics analysis skill" as "the recognition of problems in which the underlying mathematical processes are the same as a given problem but the context is different." The cognitive processes required in their assessment of science skills are much more of an admixture, but abstraction is clearly involved. Students must "know, use, and integrate" information, which entails recognizing "basic ideas in a different context"; recognizing "relationships of concepts, facts, and principles to phenomena observed and data collected"; and "generalizing; hypothesizing; interpolating and extrapolating; reasoning by analogy, induction and deduction; and synthesizing and modeling" (National Assessment of Educational Progress, 1986b, pp. 9-10).

1.5.4. The Issue of Transfer: Do Cognitive Skills Generalize?

We have seen that abstraction is a means of classification used to structure knowledge and solve problems, that it is taught in school from the lowest to the highest grade, that students learn to use abstraction across the disciplines, and that abstraction is deemed important to life beyond formal schooling. It is tempting to close this discussion of the relevance of abstraction to education without raising the issue of transfer, a topic of considerable debate. Instead of doing that, however, arguments on both sides of the debate are summarized below and my position is stated. Admittedly this settles nothing, but it does make my own orientation and assumptions explicit.

The debate on transfer can be framed in several ways, all of which are oversimplifications (and this is part of the problem). This discussion draws heavily from Perkins and Salomon's (1989) presentation of the issue, which they state as follows: Is intellectual competence more a function of having a lot of information at one's disposal, or of having skill at general problem solving strategies? Framed as a dilemma, we find that the "specialist" sits at one horn and the "generalist" sits at the other. In their sweeping overview of evidence on both sides of the issue, Perkins and Salomon (1989) discuss three arguments against the generalist's position.

The first is the *argument from expertise,* which builds on Glaser's (1984) "theory of expert problem solving." Glaser sees the difference between expert and novice problem solving as a function of acquired knowledge rather than processing capabilities. He writes that "the problem solving difficulty of novices can be attributed largely to the inadequacies of their knowledge bases and not to limitations in their processing capabilities such as the inability to use problem-solving heuristics" (Glaser, 1984, p. 99). The second argument against the generalist's position is the *argument from weak methods.* It is based on artificial intelligence research, which shows that programming general heuristic strategies into computers without including detailed databases does not lead to solutions, especially as problems become more complex. The third argument is the most direct and is appropriately called the *argument from transfer.* Simply stated, it is based on empirical studies that show that skills taught in one subject domain are not readily used in other domains.

As with all dilemmas, evidence is met with counterevidence. Clement's (1982) research shows that when experts face unfamiliar, atypical problems in their domains of specialization, they turn to general heuristic strategies. Schoenfeld (1985, p. 20) demonstrates that "heuristic instruction can yield dramatic gains in college students' mathematical problem solving" when the instruction makes "good contact with students' knowledge base in the domain." Perkins and Salomon themselves conclude, from studies showing evidence of transfer, that what is needed is *much practice* with a mode of thought in a *variety of situations*. They observe that "transfer occurs only under specific conditions, which are often not met in everyday life or laboratory experiments . . . . When the conditions *are* met, useful transfer from one context to another often occurs" (pp. 21-22).

Perkins and Salomon propose a resolution to the transfer debate in the form of a "synthesis position," which challenges the assumed polarization of general cognitive skills and factual knowledge. "There are general cognitive skills, but they always function in contextualized ways . . . [as] gripping devices for retrieving and wielding domain-specific knowledge, as hands that need pieces of knowledge to grip and wield and that need to configure . . ." (pp. 19, 23). Upon reflection it is hard to imagine how it could be otherwise; knowledge is built up through the interaction of cognition and content. Abstraction, for instance, entails the detection of similarities (the cognitive part) in otherwise distinct objects of analysis (the content part).[6]

1.6. Refining the Definition of Abstraction

This section returns to the relational definition of abstraction, which is seen as inadequate because it does not distinguish abstraction from stereotyping. A framework is proposed for distinguishing between these two modes of thought, which nevertheless share a foundation in processes of categorization and generalization. A precise definition of stereotype thinking is a necessary part of defining abstraction.

1.6.1. Undergeneralization Versus Overgeneralization

It will be recalled that a definition of relational abstraction cited early in this chapter is: "when the mind, beginning with isolated individuals, groups them together in virtue of perceived resemblances and arrives at a unity in plurality" (*Encyclopaedia Britannica,* 1919, p. 77). Similarly, in an article titled "The

[6]Cormier and Hagman (1987, p. xi) conceive of transfer quite generally as "whenever our existing knowledge, abilities, and skills affect the learning or performance of new tasks." This conception does not depend on the unrealistic expectation that if learning, or education more generally, has any effects they are immediate and direct. This mechanistic orientation is antithetical to the more developmental and ecological perspectives, which are characteristic of the learning–generalization model, and social learning theory more generally (see, e.g., Ahammer, 1973).

Psychology of Abstraction," Kelly and Krueger (1984, p. 63) assert that "countless different theories" of abstraction agree "on certain basic points":

> . . . that a crucial part of the process is the observation of similarities among objects . . . and that somehow the determinate differences among similar objects are ignored or factored out, so that objects can be seen as identical.

The fact that each of these descriptions of abstraction fails to distinguish it from the related process of *stereotyping* is revealed in the phrase "and arrives at a unity in plurality" in the first case and "so that objects can be seen as identical" in the second. It may not immediately be apparent, but stereotype thinking and abstraction are alike insofar as each involves categorization as a means of simplifying the world and imposing meaning on it. But whatever distinguishes them should be made explicit in their respective definitions.

Simply stated, abstraction and stereotyping both involve classification on the basis of similarities, but they differ with respect to the recognition of differences. In the case of stereotyping, the classification of individual cases according to a presumed group characteristic proceeds unchecked by the existence of relevant differences among members of the group. The same cannot be said of abstraction. Werner Landecker's (1982, p. 80) two-dimensional definition of abstraction makes this distinction explicit by stressing the idea of perceiving commonalties without skimming over relevant differences.

> [T]o make abstractions . . . is to recognize shared properties of different objects, but without overlooking their differences and thus overgeneralizing. Abstraction always involves a distinction between those properties that are shared by various objects and those that are not. . . . [A]bstraction is flanked by concreteness on one side and by stereotypes on the other, and has to be distinguished from both.

The unique feature of Landecker's definition is that it sets limits on seeing similarities; it appreciates the fact that generalization exists on a continuum, one extreme being undergeneralization (or concrete thinking) and the other being overgeneralization (or stereotype thinking). Landecker explicitly defines abstraction in joint contradistinction to both of these extremes. Empirically speaking, abstraction can be measured in either of two ways: (a) unidimensionally, by items that require the detection of similarities without overlooking differences in objects of analysis, or (b) multidimensionally, by one set of items specifically designed to indicate nonconcrete thinking and by another set of items designed to indicate nonstereotype thinking.

The idea that abstraction and stereotyping are related modes of thought needs to be examined in greater detail. Stereotyping has become a major concept in our culture, and much attention has been given to it in research journals, books, newspapers, and other media ever since Walter Lippmann first discussed its social significance in 1922 in a book titled *Public Opinion*. In the years since Lippmann introduced the idea of "the pictures we carry about in our heads," several different perspectives on stereotyping have evolved. We examine these next.

1.6.2. *Different Conceptions of Stereotyping*

There are three major theoretical approaches to the study of stereotypes and stereotyping (Ashmore & Del Boca, 1981). The sociological or sociocultural perspective tends to treat stereotypes as social phenomena "out there," the psychodynamic perspective focuses on stereotyping as a means of satisfying a psychological need, and the cognitive perspective treats stereotyping as a "built-in" feature of the human cognitive apparatus. After considering the strengths and weaknesses of each approach, I argue for a return to the more balanced treatment of stereotyping as found in the classic works of Lippmann (1922) and Gorden Allport (1954).

Katz and Braly (1933) were among the first proponents of the sociological perspective, from which stereotypes are understood as value-laden beliefs and ideas that are transmitted by agents of socialization (family, teachers, peers, significant others) and cultural symbols. According to this view, stereotypes originate at the dominant levels of stratification and function to promote the status quo by providing explicit or implicit rationalizations for existing (unequal) social arrangements.[7] This approach certainly provides important and valid insights, but it merely implies the emotional purposes stereotypes serve, and it neglects their cognitive foundation.

In *The Authoritarian Personality,* Adorno et al. (1950) provided an in-depth analysis of the ego-defensive dynamics that give rise to the formation of stereotypes. The idea that stereotypes are negative, which is clearly present in the sociological point of view, is part of the psychodynamic perspective as well. Stereotypes are understood as self-protective, if biased, cognitive reactions to threatening emotional states. Although this orientation comes the closest to incorporating the other two perspectives into its treatment of stereotyping, it typically under-represents the social and cognitive bases of stereotypes.

The cognitive perspective gives much credit to the view that stereotyping is the natural tendency of the human mind to form categories (see, e.g., Tajfel, 1969). The idea that categorization is a basic means for simplifying reality and creating meanings accords with Lippmann's and Allport's classic treatises but some contemporary proponents of this orientation have taken it too far. They equate stereotypes with "cognitive concepts" or "conceptual categories" (Manis, Nelson, & Shedler, 1988, p. 29, 33) or maintain that stereotypes are "not essentially different from other generalizations" (McCauley, Stitt, & Segal, 1980, p. 196). In the same vein, others conclude that the "essential defining feature of the term" is a "set of beliefs about the personal attributes of a group of people" (Ashmore & Del Boca, 1981, p. 16). These conceptions of stereotyping have gotten away from its social and emotional foundations and have abandoned its negative connotation.

---

[7]For more on this see Huber and Form's (1973) discussion of stratification and ideology, and see the sociology of knowledge literature on which their work builds.

The cognitive approach to stereotyping might more usefully relate stereotyping to generalization processes conceived of along a continuum. Such an orientation, we have seen, is provided in Landecker's definition of abstraction as "flanked by concreteness on one side and by stereotypes on the other, and . . . distinguished from both." The basic ideas to keep in mind are that generalization admits of degree and *under*generalization is equivalent to concrete thinking whereas *over*-generalization is tantamount to stereotyping.

1.6.3. A Synthesis of Views

Lippmann's (1922) and Allport's (1954) classic writings on stereotyping consider together the issues dealt with more or less separately in the three perspectives outlined above. Lippmann's interest in stereotyping was stimulated by Dewey's "problem of acquiring meaning." How do we make sense of the unfamiliar? How do we introduce definiteness and distinction and consistency and stability into what James once described as "one great blooming, buzzing confusion" of stimuli? Lippmann (1922, p. 89) observed that "modern life is hurried and multifarious. There is neither time nor opportunity for intimate acquaintance. Instead we notice a trait which marks a well known type, and fill in the rest of the picture by means of the stereotypes we carry about in our heads." Lippmann's conception of stereotyping is clearly built on a cognitive foundation, but he proceeded to consider it from the other perspectives as well.

Not only did Lippmann introduce stereotyping as a social psychological concept, but, as Allport (1954, p. 187) observed, he also originated a misconception.

> To Mr. Lippmann goes credit for establishing the conception [of stereotypes] in modern social psychology. His treatment, however excellent on the descriptive side, was somewhat loose in theory. For one thing he tends to confuse stereotype with category.

As noted above, this misconception continues today in the cognitive perspective on stereotyping. Let us, then, turn to Allport for clarification.

In his own analysis of stereotyping, Allport also placed great significance on processes of categorization.

> We said that categories assimilate as much old and new experience as possible to themselves; that they enable us quickly to identify any object that belongs to the category; that whatever belongs to a category tends to be saturated with a common emotional flavor. Finally we pointed out that categorical thinking is a natural and inevitable tendency of the human mind . . . [p. 166].

He was careful, however, to distinguish between stereotyping and categorization. Stereotypes are *grounded* in the process of categorization (as are abstractions), but they are defined as "an exaggerated belief associated with a category."

> A stereotype, then, is not a category, but often exists as a fixed mark upon the category. If I say, "All lawyers are crooked," I am expressing a stereotyped generalization about a category. The stereotype is not in itself the core of the concept. It operates, however, in such a way as to prevent differentiated thinking about the concept [p. 187].

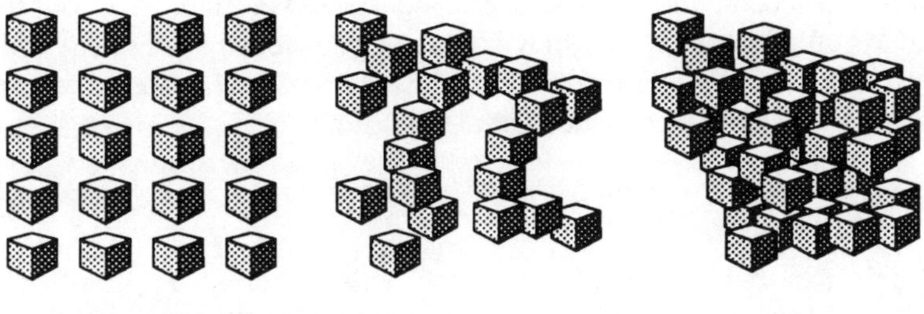

FIGURE 1.2 A graphic portrayal of the relationship between abstraction and concrete and stereotype thinking.

The definition of stereotyping as undifferentiated thinking about concepts is central to the refined definition of abstraction. The conception of stereotype thinking as overly categorical, simplistic, rigid, and inaccurate coincides with the etymology of the term, from the Greek word meaning "solid type." The French printer Didot is credited with first using the word stereotype in 1798 to refer to the inked mold that *produces an image over and over again without variation or change.* A definition of stereotyping that explicitly expresses the idea that the mind is like a rigid mold when it thinks stereotypically is: "the tendency to forget or gloss over the existence and meaning of individual differences and to force upon all members of a certain group a single 'type,' characteristic, or pattern" (Fishman, 1956, pp. 31-32).[8]

Carefully defining stereotype thinking in a manner that respects all three perspectives discussed above is a necessary part of refining the definition of abstraction. Although both modes of thought derive from categorizing and grouping objects on the basis of similarities, in the case of abstraction relevant differences are recognized, whereas in the case of stereotyping they are disregarded. Figure 1.2 portrays the conceptual relationship of abstraction to its two opposites: concrete thinking and stereotype thinking. Assume that the cubes signify individual cases or objects of analysis. The left-hand panel, composed of nonoverlapping cubes, represents concrete thinking as a particularistic mode of thought, focused almost entirely on differences, in which few if any connections or commonalities are discerned. The right-hand panel, composed of cubes packed tightly into an undifferentiated mass, represents overly categorical, stereotype thinking, in which all members of a group are seen as the same. The middle panel is composed of cubes partly linked with other cubes—to represent the detection of commonalities (nonconcrete thinking), and partly separate—to

[8]Similarly, Bettelheim and Janowitz (1964) describe stereotypes of minority group members as statements "which showed that they ignored the individual's uniquely personal characteristics."

represent the recognition of differences (nonstereotype thinking). This is how abstraction is defined: as the joint product of nonconcrete thinking and non-stereotype thinking, as the recognition of *similarities and differences* in related objects of analysis.

1.7. Chapter Summary

One might say that this chapter has been nothing but a long quest for some elusive definitions. The first leg of the journey dealt with the etymology of the term, its various literal and relational meanings, the distinction between abstraction as a mode of thought and the abstractness of subject matter, and the distinction between abstraction and the far more general notion of abstract thinking.

The next leg involved taking three perspectives on abstraction: a broad view, in which abstraction was related to major theories of intelligence since the turn of the century; an applied view, in which clinical, educational, and omnibus measures of abstraction were examined; and a microscopic view, in which abstraction was analyzed in terms of the cognitive psychological mechanics of classification and concept formation.

At that point some concrete examples of abstractions helped to show that this is a mode of thought used in everyday life, in a multitude of ways, by a variety of people; in other words, that abstraction is not merely an academic thought exercise carried out by an intellectual elite. Following this, several perspectives on the educational relevance of abstraction were taken. It was discussed initially in the context of the valued place on higher order thinking, which prompted an analysis of that notion and then a critique of it. It was argued that, certainly for analytic purposes, it is better to focus on specific modes of thought. Next the teaching of abstraction was considered in several curricular contexts, and this raised the problematic issue of the transfer of cognitive skills. Although this issue is often framed such that intellectual competence is split asunder with general thinking skills pared off against specific content knowledge, these are analytic concepts rather than separate empirical entities. Perkins and Salomon's "synthesis position"—the reasonable, research-based conclusion that transfer does occur with much practice in a wide variety of situations—was adopted, as was their useful metaphor that cognitive skills function "as general gripping devices that need pieces of knowledge to grip and wield and that need to configure" information. The conception of abstraction depends on process (the detection of similarities) as well as content (among distinct objects of analysis).

The final phase of this quest involved an important refinement of the relational definition of abstraction because it did not explicitly distinguish this mode of thought from stereotyping. Using a framework in which generalization is conceived of along a continuum (as suggested by Landecker's definition of abstraction), it was possible to identify concrete thinking as equivalent to undergeneralization, stereotyping as tantamount to overgeneralization, and abstraction in contradistinction to them both.

2
Abstraction Over the Life Course: Developmental and Methodological Concerns

2.1. Introduction

With abstraction defined and conceptually clarified, we may now proceed to think about the development of this mode of thought over the life course. The first thing to establish is that abstraction is an integral part of intellectual growth in the first two decades of life. Whereas quite a lot of theory and empirical work concerns cognitive development in youth, much less research attention is focused on the much longer period of adulthood. Thus, certain that abstraction improves with age early in life, we shall concentrate on issues surrounding its development throughout the adult years. Does abstraction tend to level off in adulthood and then decline during the later years of life? Or does abstraction remain stable throughout adulthood for most people? Or does it begin to decline soon after biological maturity? These are deceptively simple questions. The full extent to which they can be answered here will not be known until the fourth, empirical chapter of this book. This chapter examines some of the methodological issues that arise in the study of adult intellectual development. We will see that the way in which one sets out to answer the above questions can lead to mistaken conclusions. By taking these spurious sources of influence into account, we should be in a better position to evaluate the genuine relationship between abstraction and age.

2.2. Abstraction and Cognitive Growth in Childhood

Infants are not born with the ability for abstraction nor does it appear all at once. Simple cognitive functions develop as a result of the joint influence of biological maturation and experience, more advanced cognitive functions evolve from more basic ones, and complex systems of knowledge develop out of simpler ones. In the beginning the infant is said to be "dependent exclusively on stimulus input," but with time his behavior becomes "guided by rules that enable him to combine perceptual information with information from memory" (Bowlby, 1980, p. 426). Goldstein (1963, p. viii) makes the same point, but with explicit reference to the concrete/abstract dimension: The infant "exists on the concrete level alone . . . [having come] into the world as a very limited organism, particularly since his abstract capacity is not yet developed." Goldstein (pp. 59–60) elaborates:

> Now I am very anxious not to be misunderstood at this point because what I am about to say concerns the most important problem in our attempt to characterize human nature on the basis of our findings . . . . In "concrete" performances a reaction is determined directly by a stimulus . . . [whereas] in "abstract" performances an action is not determined directly and immediately by a stimulus configuration but by the account of the situation which the individual gives to himself. The performance is thus more a primary action than a mere reaction, and it is a totally different way of coming to terms with the outside world.

Both Bowlby and Goldstein characterize cognitive development as the transition from concrete to abstract thinking, with the latter understood quite generally as any kind of thought-mediated action. This reflects the centrality of abstraction, conceived of in its literal sense, to the development of more advanced cognitive functions and more complex knowledge structures. To underscore the relevance of relational abstraction (which involves the additional process of comparing mental representations) to cognitive development, we turn next to a broader and more explicitly developmental framework. It will show that relational abstraction, too, appears quite early in life and is a basic part of cognitive development.

Piagetian theory (Brief, 1983; Gregory, 1987; Inhelder & Piaget, 1958; Piaget, 1981, Piaget, 1965) traces cognitive development from the primitive and utterly concrete nature of experience in early childhood—the barrage of sensation infants surely experience—through a series of stages to more advanced cognitive capacities. During infancy, cognitive activity is limited to sensory and motoric inputs and outputs. By around 2 years of age and thereafter, the developing child forms mental representations of features of the environment and performs basic cognitive operations on them, such as identifying what two or more things have in common. For example, Piaget showed that whereas the conservation of matter[1] is not typically within the preoperational child's conceptual abilities, it is learned during this period of concrete operations. To see the prevalence of this form of abstraction in children's cognition one need only call to mind the familiar Seseme Street song that begins "Which of these things is not like the other . . ."

Biological maturation, linguistic development, and social experience facilitate the transition to the period of formal operations around early adolescence. Piaget describes formal operations as the skillful coordination of cognitive actions (such as logical reasoning and deductive thinking) on mental representations. A defining feature of the period of formal operations is the use of hierarchically advanced cognitive functions. Indeed, Piaget's stage theory portrays the development of thought processes as progressing from simpler to more advanced operations. Thus, object constancy and conservation of matter do not appear in the preoperational child, inductive processes appear after constancy and conservation but before deductive skills, and such logical operations as transitivity and reversal are exclusive to the period of formal operations.

---

[1]Clearly, relational abstraction is involved in the realization that two breakers of radically different shape nevertheless hold the same volume of fluid.

In the Piagetian scheme of cognitive development, relational abstraction is a relatively early appearing concrete operation that also combines with other components of cognitive functioning to produce more advanced modes of thought (such as reasoning by analogy) in the period of formal operations. But abstraction remains a basic means of operating on intellectual content at all levels of complexity. As we saw earlier, because abstraction is defined as classification on the basis of similarities and differences, we can infer that it is used to draw generalizations and to form new concepts in relation to old ones. Thus, it is central to assimilation and accommodation, processes that are basic to Piaget's theory of intellectual growth.

2.3. Intellectual Decline in Adulthood?

If the first two decades of life are a time of intellectual growth, it has long been thought that adulthood is a time of intellectual decline. For example, Byron penned:

> Years steal
> Fire from the mind, as vigor from the limb:
> And life's enchanted cup but sparkles near the brim.
> (Childe Harold, Canto III. St. 8.)

The reference to old age as a second childhood can be traced at least as far back as to the following well known passage from Shakespeare's *As You Like It.*

> All the world's a stage,
> And all the men and women merely players;
> They have their exits and their entrances;
> And one man in his time plays many parts,
> His acts being seven ages. . . .
>
> Last scene of all,
> That ends this strange eventful history,
> Is second childishness and mere oblivion,
> Sans teeth, sans eyes, sans taste, sans every thing.
> (Act II. Sc. 7. L. 139.)

Many of us know some elderly people who, by example, confirm these notions, and others who, being mentally astute and wise, contradict them. There is no simple answer to the question whether intellectual functioning declines in adulthood, yet the topic is of direct interest to us all. It encompasses a number of issues, each quite complicated in itself: (a) Is decline the rule for all intellectual abilities (i.e., is it *universal*), or do some types of intellectual functioning remain stable, or even increase with age?; (b) Is decline the rule for most people (i.e., is it *normative*), or is there marked individual variation?; (c) Is decline irreversible, or is there substantial *plasticity* in intellectual change in adulthood?; and (d) Is evidence of decline or stability partly a function of the method of data collection used to arrive at answers to these questions? The latter issue cuts across the others, thus providing a window onto each. Therefore, we will carefully examine it in the following sections.

2.3.1. Evidence of Decline from Cross-Sectional Data

The data analyzed in this study, which were collected from a sample of 615 adults living in a large metropolitan area, are described in detail in chapter 4. In anticipation of this discussion, the relationship between age and abstraction is displayed in Figure 2.1. In this figure average abstraction scores are plotted at each age from 18 to 88 years (the age of the oldest respondent), which indicates an inverse relation between the two variables: abstraction decreases as age increases. This simple relationship indicates that decline begins early and is unrelenting.[2]

This outcome is consistent with results from previous studies; for example, according to Salthouse (1982, p. 93), "the prevailing opinion is that thinking becomes less abstract and more concrete with increased age." Likewise, Bromley (1974, p. 188) reports that "the tendency for older people to become less capable of thinking in abstract terms" is supported by research based on the Similarities subtest of the WAIS and Raven's PM. It is believed that this deficit is "not simply a difficulty in generating abstractions, but also in recognizing them among more concrete alternatives" (Salthouse, 1982, p. 94). The same trend—intellectual decline with advancing age—is found in a number of cross-sectional studies of abstraction-related cognitive functions, for example, categorizing and conceptualizing (Cicirelli, 1976; Kogan, 1974), classifying (Denney, 1974; Reese & Rodeheaver, 1985), deductive reasoning (Arenberg, 1968; Hartley, 1981), generalizing (Botwanick, 1978), and others (Arbuckle, Gold, & Andres, 1986; Botawanick, 1977; Parks, Mitchell, & Perlmutter, 1986).

2.3.2. The Deficit Model

Several decades ago, in a review article on adult intellectual development, Jones (1959, p. 700, quoted in Labouvie-Vief, 1985, p. 500) described the then popular "hill" or "deficit" model:

> In the first two decades [of life] the effects [of aging on intelligence] are chiefly positive and are defined in terms of growth or maturation. In later maturity negative changes are apparent with progressive age reductions in functional efficiency.

More recently, Labouvie-Vief (1985, p. 500) observed that this view is consistent with the Piagetian and Freudian approaches to cognitive development, which "define psychological growth as nearly coterminous with physical maturity" and "visualize its completion in late adolescence."

---

[2]The product–moment correlation between age and abstraction is −.30. A one-way analysis of variance resulted in an eta-squared of .095, which is not significantly different from the square of the correlation coefficient. This shows that there is not a significant amount of nonlinearity in the age-abstraction relationship.

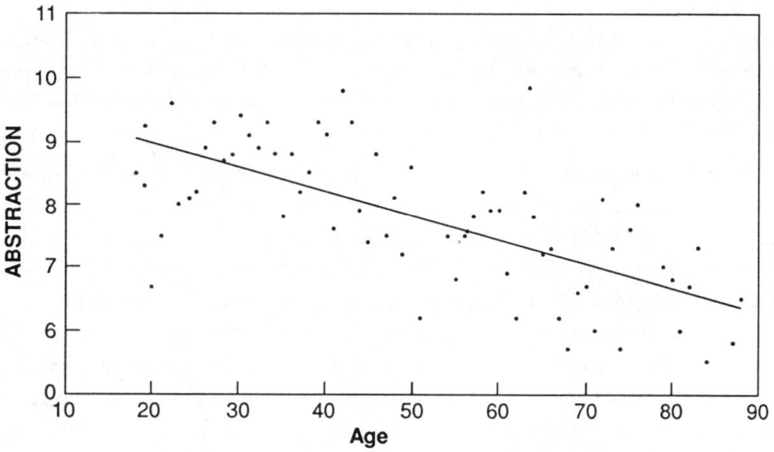

FIGURE 2.1. Abstraction by Age (N = 615)

The neural noise theory, which complements the deficit model, attributes age-related decline in intellectual functioning to biological maturation. Its thesis is that decreased neural efficiency is caused by loss of neurons, decreased cerebral blood flow, and increased randomness in neural activity. It posits that such degenerative processes cause a reduced "signal-to-noise ratio within the nervous system" as early as the third decade of life (Salthouse, 1982, p. 46).

Advocates of the deficit model see aging as a retrogressive process "that proceeds from higher to lower levels of functioning" and that "involves the loss of the hierarchic integration of functions." Thus, it is believed, "the aging individual . . . functions at a more concrete, lower level of organization" (Labouvie-Vief, 1985, pp. 502–503). It may be recalled from the review of abstraction measures designed for clinical purposes in the previous chapter that retrogradation to a concrete level of intellectual functioning has often been taken as the sine qua non of mental impairment. Indeed, a parallel between cognitive aging and pathology has been codified in Rubinstein's so-called "law of regression of intellectual functioning in pathology and aging" (Labouvie-Vief, 1985, p. 503).

Since the 1970s the deficit model has been criticized with increasing vigor due to: (a) greater awareness of the limitations of cross-sectional methods in the study of human development, and (b) greater awareness of the relevance of the social context in which aging occurs. Too often in the past the type of relationship observed in Figure 2.1 was taken at face value as evidence in support of the deficit model and the neural noise theory. Such conclusions are premature, as Labouvie-Vief (1985, p. 503) explains:

> [The deficit model] suggest[s] that cognitive aging results, in part, from biological (presumably, largely genetic) limitations on an organism's fluidity or its capacity for plasticity. The assumption of such limitations may be based on an artifact, however, as research has often failed to account for the multitude of ways in which individual development is influenced by socio-cultural factors.

She then asks, somewhat rhetorically: "[A]re we to adhere . . . to the notion that [intellectual] deficits are normative and universal, or are we to explain them by variations in the contexts in which individuals age?"

This explanatory orientation, in which social factors are advanced as causes of variation in intellectual functioning, provides an important perspective. First, differences in social experience certainly seem to help account for individual differences among same-aged people at different times in the life course, as Labouvie-Vief suggests. Second, it is likely that age-related differences in intellectual functioning observed in cross-sectional studies are due at least in part to birth cohort differences in social experiences. This second consideration raises a number of important design and methodological issues to be discussed next in detail.

2.4. Mistaking Cohort Differences for Age Effects in Cross-Sectional Data

A *cohort* is a set of individuals who pass a crucial stage at approximately the same time (Carlsson & Karlsson, 1970). Members of a birth cohort are in the unique position of experiencing the same sequence of historic events at the same time in the life cycle. It follows that at any given period of time, age and birth cohort membership are in perfect agreement; that is, older people were born earlier and younger people were born later. This direct correspondence between age and time of birth is a potential source of confusion in analyses of cross-sectional data because effects of the different social conditions experienced by different birth cohorts can be mistakenly attributed to the effect of age. Much of the evidence for the deficit model is based on cross-sectional data in which change is inferred from age differences without taking into account the effects of different social conditions experienced by members of different birth cohorts.

The simple fact that formal schooling was less available to members of earlier birth cohorts should serve to caution one against automatically interpreting age-related deficits in intellectual functioning as evidence of mental impairment due to biological aging. When today's elders were youths, primary education was not mandatory, secondary education was not universally available, and only a select few attended college. Thus, simply observing the diminution of intellectual functioning across the adult years in cross-sectional data is hardly sufficient to conclude that biological aging causes intellectual decline.

Age and cohort effects on intellectual functioning can be inter-related in rather complex ways. For example, a decreasing rate of morbidity (due to improved sanitation, health care, or preventative health practices) is likely to result in less of a negative impact of aging on intellectual functioning over time. Another form of interaction is when the effects of social conditions underlying cohort differences vary depending on the time of life in which they are experienced, as described in the following passage by Carlsson and Karlsson (1970, pp. 710–711).

> With increasing age people become less likely to change; in its later life each birth cohort reflects, therefore, largely the conditions prevailing during its formative earlier years. Changing conditions will become visible most directly and most quickly in the behavior of young people, late cohorts, and much less in the behavior of earlier cohorts, that is, among middle-aged or old people [see also Alwin, Cohen, & Newcomb, in press; Mannheim, 1952; Ryder, 1965].

The same idea is stated in more general terms by Riley (1987, p. 7) when she observes that because society changes, people in different cohorts age in different ways.

There is ample evidence of cohort differences in intellectual functioning. For example, when the results from the first administration of the Army Alpha Test are compared with those from another administration given 30 years later, it is learned that the average scores of same-age adults were higher for those who were tested later (Brody & Brody, 1976, pp. 164–165). Another well known case is reported by Schaie (1983a), who finds statistically significant cohort differences in a comparison of three cross-sectional data sets collected at 7-year intervals. Elsewhere, Schaie (1979) reports that between-cohort differences in the level of performance of same-age adults are as large as the age changes revealed when following a single cohort longitudinally. These and similar findings lead Baltes, Dittmann-Kohli, and Dixon (1984, p. 40) to the following conclusion:

> Because such cohort differences for same-age adults are not likely to reflect biological or genetic differences between generations, the conclusion that they are largely related to differing environmental conditions (e.g., life histories) for the cohorts studied seems warranted.

Growing awareness of the problems inhering in cross-sectional designs as well as the advantages of longitudinal data in the study of human development has resulted in enthusiasm for longitudinal research. The following section considers the methodological advantages of this approach to the study of intellectual functioning across adulthood, some findings from such studies, and finally, the limitations of this approach.

2.5. The Longitudinal Study of Adult Intellectual Development

The longitudinal approach to the study of human development is generally regarded as superior to the cross-sectional approach (Schaie, 1983, pp. 1–4). Single-cohort longitudinal studies incorporate a test-retest strategy that permits age to vary while time of birth remains constant. Thus, observed age differences cannot be attributed to cohort effects for the simple reason that cohort membership is fixed.

Although the single-cohort longitudinal design avoids confounding age and cohort effects by observing change within individuals, it is susceptible to confounding age and time-of-measurement, or period, effects. That is, when following a panel through time, although it may be observed that intellectual functioning changes as individuals grow older, time (or history) changes too. Thus, age differences observed in single cohort longitudinal data reflect "aging intermingled with social change" (Riley, 1973, p. 43). Schaie (1983, p. 7) elaborates as follows:

> The presence of period effects related to the dependent variable of interest will render estimates of age effects internally invalid. These period effects may either mimic or suppress maturational changes occurring over a particular age span, depending on whether age and time-of-measurement effects covary positively or negatively.

Sophisticated analytic methods (or "accounting techniques") have been employed in the attempt to pull apart age, period, and cohort effects, but without the aid of certain theory-based assumptions none has been successful (Fienberg & Mason, 1985; Glenn, 1981a, 1981b). The best available solution for the *identification* problem (the fact that age, period, and cohort, each taken separately, is defined by the other two) is the intensive cross-sequential longitudinal design.[3]

Most current longitudinal studies fall short of this mark, but they do provide information that we should take into account here. The following subsections summarize findings from four longitudinal studies of adult intellectual functioning chosen for their relevance to the present work. They are selected from seven major longitudinal studies that, according to Schaie (1983, p. 12), "probably represent the bulk of work on what is securely known about age changes in psychological variables from young adulthood into old age."[4] Each summary includes information about the design and time frame of the study, its sample, the dependent variables of interest, and pertinent findings.

---

[3]For a brief explanation and discussion of various sequential designs, see Schaie (1983, p. 7–12) and Horn and Donaldson (1976, pp. 702–705). "The term 'sequence' merely implies that the required sampling frame involves a sequence of samples taken across several measurement occasions" (Schaie, 1983, p. 8). To realize the cross-sequential design "it is necessary to sample cross-sectionally in the usual manner and to follow up the individuals of this sample in the manner of longitudinal study. In [this] most efficient design there is an additional requirement that at each follow-up, a sample be drawn of individuals the same age as the youngest cohort in the first sampling" (Horn & Donaldson, 1976, p. 703).

[4]The following studies were omitted from consideration here because their psychological variables are not particularly relevant to abstraction: the Bonn Longitudinal Study on Aging, the Baltimore Longitudinal Study of Aging, and the AT&T Longitudinal Studies of Managers.

2.5.1. The Iowa State Study

Data were collected using the Army Alpha test from a single cohort of male college freshman in 1919 who were followed up in 1950 and again in 1961. In one of the most recent analyses of these data, Cunningham and Birren (1980) adopted Guilford's (1954) three factor (verbal, numerical, and relations) model of intelligence to index the eight subtests of the Army Alpha Test. Separate analyses of each factor produced mixed results, but when the factors were combined into a single index of general intellectual functioning the following conclusions were drawn:

> Clearly, the results contradict the kinds of early declines indicated by the early, well-replicated cross-sectional studies. The results suggest peak performance and the beginning of declines of overall intellectual functioning roughly in the age decade of the 50s for this elite sample. The losses appear to be small and probably are not of much practical significance until at least age 60 [Cunningham & Owens, 1983, p. 34].

Note that two qualifications detract significantly from the generalizability of these conclusions: (a) the timing of decline differed across the three factors, and (b) the population of inference is limited. These shortcomings are considered more fully below.

2.5.2. The Aging Twins Study

In 1947 the New York State Psychiatric Institute collected psychometric data for the first wave of its Study of Aging Twins. Initially, 134 pairs of twins (white residents from the state of New York aged 60 years or older) were given a battery of tests designed to measure intellectual functioning. The battery consisted primarily of five subtests from the Wechsler-Bellevue scale: Similarities, Digits Forward and Backward, Digit Symbol Substitution, and Block Design. Surviving twin pairs were retested in 1955, 1957, 1967 (when the average age was about 85), and for the last time in 1973. According to Jarvik and Bank (1983, p. 44) the results of this study indicate "general stability of nonspeeded cognitive performance to age 75 and possibly even longer." Indeed, the authors report that a number of abilities declined only in the ninth decade of life.

2.5.3. The Seattle Longitudinal Study

Schaie's Seattle Longitudinal Study (SLS) has produced a cornucopia of important data and research pertaining to adult intellectual development. His methodological, analytic, and substantive contributions are generally recognized as "pioneering" (e.g., Baltes et al., 1984, p. 40; Horn & Donaldson, 1976, p. 703). The SLS began in 1956 and spanned a 21-year period during which time there were 4 testings, each separated by 7 years. The population frame was obtained by random selection from an age- and sex-stratified list of members of the Group Health Cooperative of Puget Sound (the first broad-based health maintenance organization in the United States). The first sample consisted of 500 people aged

20 to 70 years. The three follow-up studies retested subjects from this sample, thus providing the longitudinal database. In addition, four cross-sectional samples were randomly selected, one at each time of measurement. As mentioned above, this cross-sequential strategy provides the best available means for analyzing age, cohort, and period effects.

Schaie used the Primary Mental Abilities test battery to measure intelligence. He further consolidated Thurstone's 11-factor structure into five major abilities: verbal meaning, reasoning, space, number, and word fluency. At times Schaie combines these to form two indices: Intellectual Ability (paralleling the conventional IQ test), and Educational Aptitude (a predictor of performance in educational settings).

Evidence from the SLS suggests that there is no normative decline in general intelligence until the seventh or eighth decade (Baltes et al., 1984, p. 40; Labouvie-Vief, 1985, p. 505). Schaie (1983b, p. 127) summarizes the findings as follows:

> At the risk of possible overgeneralization, it is my general conclusion that reliably replicable age changes in psychometric abilities of more than trivial magnitude cannot be demonstrated prior to age 60, but that reliable decrement can be shown to have occurred for all abilities by age 74. . . . It is typically the period of the late 60s and the 70s during which many individuals seem to experience significant ability decrement. Even so, it is typically only by age 81 that one can show that the average older person will fall below the middle range of performance for young adults.

2.5.4. The Duke Longitudinal Studies

The Duke studies were broadly multidisciplinary and "focused on providing information that describes normal aging during the later half of the life span" (Siegler, 1983, p. 136). In the first of two data sets the initial wave of data was collected in 1955 on 267 subjects. The tenth and final wave was collected in 1976 from only 42 people. In the second study, data were collected four times between 1968 and 1976, from 502 subjects initially and from 331 subjects at the time of the last testing. In both studies the WAIS was used to measure intellectual functioning; the first employed the long form, the second, the short form. Considered together, findings from the Duke Longitudinal Studies indicate that the maintenance of health is positively related to stability in intellectual performance (Siegler, 1983, p. 163) and that the intellectual performance of healthy respondents does not decline until the 70s (Schaie, 1983, p. 16).[5]

---

[5]Measures of health included indices of the integrity of the central nervous system, the immune system, and the cardiovascular system.

It is interesting to note some of the findings from the Duke studies concerning the inevitability of decline and the form it takes over time. In a study of "terminal change" in intellectual functioning, three quarters of the sample declined before death. Eighty percent of those who decline show primarily linear decline (Siegler, 1983, p. 151).

2.5.5. *What Longitudinal Research Suggests about the Relationship between Age and Abstraction*

Many conclusions drawn from the longitudinal studies described here support the view that general intelligence stays on an even keel well into adulthood and declines only late in life. On the basis of this generalization we might infer that a similar pattern of stability exists for abstraction. We would hypothesize that the discrepancy between this presumed pattern of stability and the sharply negative association observed in Figure 2.1 is entirely a function of variation in cohort-related factors. That would be premature, however, for we have yet to consider the shortcomings of current longitudinal studies of intellectual development in adulthood. Neither have we taken into account the fact that the results summarized in this section concern general intellectual functioning, whereas it is known that different subtests have differential patterns of decline. Each of these issues is taken up in respective sections below.

2.6. Shortcomings of Longitudinal Designs and Studies

Although longitudinal strategies enable researchers to circumvent problems inhering in cross-sectional designs, the longitudinal method itself is subject to limitations that may bias results in favor of intellectual stability. Already we have seen that one threat to the internal validity of traditional longitudinal designs is the obfuscation of historical (period) and maturational (age) effects. As stated in an earlier passage quoted from Schaie, period effects may either mimic or suppress maturational changes over a particular age span.

Consider the following example of how historical change can misleadingly contribute to the appearance of maturational change.[6] In the mid-1970s, researchers at the Institute for Social Research of the University of Michigan began a national longitudinal study of high school seniors' marijuana use. The results from this single-cohort longitudinal study indicate that use of this drug declines with age. Over the same period of time, annual cross-sectional studies of high school seniors' marijuana use were also conducted. These studies reveal that marijuana use peaked in the late 1970s and has been declining since then. Thus, what appears to be an effect of aging from the longitudinal perspective is actually determined by conditions unique to the time period in which the study was conducted. This illustrates that social factors cannot always be ruled out as the source of age-related stability or change in single-cohort longitudinal studies.

Two other interrelated problems that beset longitudinal studies—sample attrition and the nonrepresentativeness of samples—tend to contribute to the impression of intellectual stability. Sample attrition occurs when members of the original study group are not available for subsequent measurement(s). Whereas

[6]Conveyed in an informal presentation by Jerald Bachman (1987).

lack of interest and geographic mobility are two common causes of attrition, longitudinal studies that follow subjects into old age are also vulnerable to the effects of morbidity and mortality on their samples. It is important to realize that (problems of sample size and statistical power aside) attrition is a problem only when it is selective; that is, when a factor leading to dropout is also related to a dependent variable of interest. In other words, if people exhibit different patterns of intellectual development over the life course and if the "decliners" have a higher dropout rate, then results will be biased toward stability.

The most direct evidence that any of the longitudinal studies discussed above keep stable subjects and lose decliners is reported by Jarvik and Bank (1983, pp. 46–51) with regard to the Aging Twins Study. They related the concept of "critical loss"—measured by change in score consistency over the first three testing periods on three "critical tests" (including the Similarities subtest of the WAIS)—to attrition from death:

> Returning (post hoc) to the subsample of twins with complete data on each of the three critical tests for each of the three test rounds, 22 of the 26 twins without critical loss were survivors, while 7 of the 8 twins with critical loss were deceased. It is worth noting that the deceased twins with critical loss constituted the youngest subgroup [Jarvik & Bank, 1983, p. 48].

This is consistent with findings from the Duke Longitudinal Studies suggesting that the maintenance of health is positively related to stability in intellectual performance. Similarly, it is reported that 10 years after the Duke studies began, 39% of the high IQ subjects had dropped out as compared with 51% of the middle IQ subjects and 72% of the low IQ subjects (Siegler, 1983, p. 149). These results foster a certain degree of wariness for it appears that longitudinal studies give the impression of intellectual stability in part because subjects with relatively flat intellectual trajectories remain in the study while decliners drop out of it. Attrition due to disinterest or geographic mobility can be avoided to a degree, but attrition due to morbidity and mortality cannot.

Even without the problem of attrition, the lack of representativeness of the samples of many longitudinal studies of intellectual development is a problem with important ramifications (see, e.g., Horn & Donaldson, 1976, or, more generally, Schooler, 1989). If intellectual functioning is influenced by cultural and structural factors that are determined by position in the social structure,[7] then studies with narrow populations of inference suffer from problems of external validity (e.g., Kish, 1987). Thus, it is relevant to note that even Schaie's acclaimed Seattle Longitudinal Study employed samples drawn (albeit randomly) from a self-selected population frame consisting of people who joined the Puget Sound Group Health Cooperative.

In sum, these limitations caution that some results from longitudinal studies of intellectual change in adulthood are likely to be biased in the opposite direction of cross-sectional studies on this topic. Confounded age and period effects,

---

[7]Evidence in support of this basic proposition is reviewed in the following chapter.

attrition related to the dependent variable(s) of the study, nonrepresentativeness of (often) elite samples, even the tendency to draw generalizations from a relatively narrow age range (Salthouse, 1982, pp. 75–77)—each of these factors may promote the appearance of intellectual stability until old age in longitudinal studies.

A simple summation of the opposing biases characteristic of cross-sectional studies (exaggerated decline) and longitudinal studies (exaggerated stability) that investigate adult intellectual development leads to the conclusion that the average trend in general intellectual functioning in the population at large is somewhere between early linear decline and stability until old age. But the more interesting and important issues and questions concern the existence of and reasons for differences across people, across subtests of intellectual functioning, and across the life span. We have already seen that individuals differ in the degree to which intellectual functioning remains stable or changes across the adult years. Next we consider the implications of longitudinal research findings of differential patterns of decline across subtests for the study of adult intellectual functioning.

2.7. Differential Patterns of Development

The existence of high correlations among subtests of intellectual functioning is often cited as justification for the analysis of general intellectual functioning based on composite indices. Yet the underlying issue, described here by Terman (1906; quoted in Gould, 1981, p. 175), has been the subject of debate for a long time: "Is intellectual ability a bank account, on which we can draw for any desired purpose, or is it rather a bundle of separate drafts, each drawn for a specific purpose and inconvertible?". In the first chapter we considered this issue from three distinct yet related perspectives: from the reification fallacy point of view, from cognitive science and information processing orientations, and in the context of the debate on transfer. Here, the issue arises again, but now in the context of a methodological problem.

The problem can be briefly described as follows: On the one hand, highly correlated subtests support a unitary conception of intelligence. On the other hand, there is considerable evidence that subtests have different developmental trends, which suggests a pluralist orientation. Salthouse (1982, p. 54) elaborates:

> At any given age the various subtests are generally highly correlated with one another. This is rather surprising in view of the diverse nature of many of the subtests, and it has been taken as evidence for the existence of a common factor of general intelligence.

However, he also explains:

> The discovery that the component abilities of an intelligence test do exhibit differential age trends was one of the earliest, and is still one of the best supported findings in the field of adult developmental psychology. . . . [T]hat the various subtests exhibit quite different developmental trends, seems to suggest that intelligence is not unitary and that there are different, functionally independent, forms of intelligence.

The fact of differential patterns of decline virtually decides the issue for the scholar of adult intellectual development. Correlations indicate relative position on scales, and thus, while correlations among various measures of intellectual functioning remain high across the life course, the particular skills may either decrease, remain stable, or even increase. Information about differential patterns of change is lost when analyses are based on composite indices only. Salthouse (1982, p. 54) draws the same conclusion, as have others:

> While the composite intelligence score has some justification for being considered a measure of global intelligence, its meaning may be substantially different at various portions of the life span because the same composite score can be produced by many different combinations of subtest scores. If some of the subtest abilities are declining with age while others are improving, the composite measure might be very misleading in indicating no age differences in overall intelligence. To the extent that the various subtests differ in their developmental trends, therefore, it seems unreasonable to attempt to make interpretations about the relationship between age and intelligence on the basis of a single composite measure of intelligence.

It was noted in chapter 1 that the distinction between intellectual abilities that decline with age and those that improve or remain stable is the basis for the theory of crystallized and fluid intelligence. It is said that the first mental abilities lost to aging are the most complex or hierarchically superior operations. More specifically, proponents of this theory maintain that "the primary deficits brought about by aging lie in the abstraction and integration of novel information," and that aging of the memory system is "due to failure to utilize more abstract codes." From this perspective, then, "the aging individual . . . functions at a more concrete, lower level of organization" (Labouvie-Vief, 1985. p. 502). If indeed it is true that fluid abilities, or those that typically decline with age, do entail the most "hierarchically superior operations," bear in mind that it does not follow that abstraction, conceived of as seeing similarities without disregarding differences, is among this group. The confusion here seems to be misconstruing abstraction as necessarily complex. We have seen that this is probably due, at least in part, to confounding abstraction as defined here with modes of thought that operate at high levels of abstractness. Abstraction is a relatively simple, "concrete operation" (to use Piagetian terminology) and there is no a priori reason to peg it as a mode of fluid intelligence that is expected to decline with age.

2.8. Chapter Summary and Directions for Empirical Research

Figure 2.1 portrays a sharp linear decline in abstraction across the adult years in a representative sample of adults from a large metropolitan region. This trend, and similar findings from other cross-sectional studies of adult intellectual functioning, supports the deficit model, which predicts intellectual decline with age. However, because the cross-sectional design confounds cohort differences in social experiences with maturational change, the relationship between age and abstraction displayed in Figure 2.1 must be interpreted with caution.

Longitudinal studies of adult intellectual development—which tend to support the view that intellectual decline in adulthood is a "myth"—get around the confound of age and cohort effects, but most of them are subject to the confuscation of historical and maturational effects. Other problems that beset longitudinal studies are the attrition of subjects (with decliners dropping out at a higher rate than others) and the nonrepresentativeness of samples (which raises questions about external validity). We have considered how these limitations bias results in the direction of stability. But these limitations aside, the longitudinal study of adult intellectual development makes significant contributions to the study of intellectual development across the life course. Longitudinal results typically challenge the view that intellectual decline is universal (occurs across most abilities) and normative (happens to most people as a natural result of aging). A mixture of longitudinal and cross-sectional methods is the best design for collecting data on adult intellectual development.

We can conclude that the study of the development of *general* intelligence is misguided because there is substantial evidence that there are different developmental trends among subtests and these subtests are combined in composite indices. Developmental studies of specific intellectual functions—such as abstraction—are needed.

What are the implications of these various methodological considerations for the present study of abstraction and age? Does the fact that *only* cross-sectional data are available to evaluate this relationship mean that we are hopelessly mired in the age-cohort confound? The answer to this question is an unqualified "no." Not to downplay the problems we will face in using cross-sectional data, let us acknowledge, together with Glenn (1981b, p. 362), that "the recognition of the hazards of inferring age effects from cross-sectional data [is] all too often accompanied by an unwarranted enthusiasm for longitudinal data."

> All too often, students of aging now fail to recognize that cross-sectional data properly analyzed and supplemented with information from other sources can often provide more nearly conclusive evidence about the effects of aging than can any other one kind of data.

The key to "proper analysis" is to realize that the identification problem is not insurmountable. It is true that accounting methods alone cannot pull apart age, period, and cohort effects (in cohort analysis), age and cohort effects (in cross-sectional analysis), and age and period effects (in single-cohort longitudinal analysis). But as Riley (1973, p. 47) says, "the researcher can circumvent the identification fallacy by recognizing age and date for what they are . . . [namely] mere surrogates for other variables in the emerging sociology of age."

At several times in this chapter we have had occasion to observe that social experiences have differential effects on individuals' psychological functioning. At present this statement is too general to be useful in empirical research on the sociology of age and intellectual functioning. Therefore, the following chapter considers both a number of specific social contexts that influence abstraction-related modes of psychological functioning and the ways in which these effects are transmitted (cf. House, 1977).

3
The Social Bases of Intellectual Functioning

3.1. Introduction

Let us recognize from the beginning that biology constrains and conditions intellectual functioning and development and probably helps to account for some measure of differences that exist across individuals. Let us also recognize, however, that there remains a great deal of variation in intellectual functioning—across the life course, social strata, societies, and history—that can be analyzed as a function of the social and physical environments in which development occurs.

The writings of Durkheim on suicide, Weber on the protestant ethic, Marx on alienation, and Mannheim on ideology contain important sociological insights into the study of psychological differences across social groups and how such variation evolves. This chapter focuses on the common theme, that runs through diverse literatures, of the socioenvironmental determination of intellectual functioning and in so doing it responds to three broad questions. One, how does abstraction relate to cognitive outcomes that have attracted the attention of sociologists? Two, what type of environmental conditions facilitate intellectual functioning? And three, what processes link features of physical and social environments to psychological outcomes?

3.2. Ethnocentrism, Prejudice, and Abstraction

Research on ethnocentrism and prejudice, stimulated by the events of the Second World War, bears directly on our interest in the social development of abstraction. Ethnocentrism is the attitude or belief that one's own racial, ethnic, religious, or some other type of group is inherently superior to other groups (Sumner, 1906). The production of such an attitude entails stereotype thinking because traits are rigidly attributed to individuals on the basis of their group membership, and if variation among individuals within a group is recognized at all, it is disregarded. Moreover, by using one's own group as the standard against which all other groups are discriminated and then dismissed as inferior, the ethnocentric thinker is oblivious to commonalities between groups and their members. Thus, ethnocentrism also entails concrete thinking and may be characterized as the logical error of "misplaced concreteness" as depicted by Alfred North Whitehead (1948, p. 52). Considered jointly, the cognitive mechanics underlying ethnocentrism involve *within-group* stereotype thinking (seeing all members of a given group as the same) and *between-group* concrete thinking (seeing no similarities in members across groups). In brief, ethnocentrism is the failure to exercise abstraction in the domain of intergroup relations.

These conceptual relationships are supported by empirical research. For example, Rokeach (1948, p. 259) concludes from a crafty set of experimental studies that "the mode of thought of the ethnocentric person is more concrete in nature, whereas the mode of thought of the nonethnocentric person in solving problems is more abstract in nature." Similarly, Arnhoff (1956) shows that ethnocentrism is related to overgeneralization, defined as "the failure to note distinguishing characteristics" (p. 138) (which is equivalent to our conception of stereotyping). He observes in a sample of nursing students that scores on a stimulus generalization test and the California E (ethnocentrism) scale correlated at .44.

Not surprisingly, ethnocentrism and its underlying cognitive mechanics—concrete and stereotype thinking—are also related to the concept of prejudice. Indeed, Rokeach (1948), for one, does not conceive of these modes of thought as isolated phenomena within the personality, but rather as indicative of "generalized mental rigidity." In a now dated statement, Gordon Allport (1954, pp. 376–377) elaborates on this in *The Nature of Prejudice:*

> One of the most important psychological discoveries of recent years is that the dynamics of prejudice tend to parallel the dynamics of cognition. That is to say, the style of thinking that is characteristic of prejudice is a reflection, by and large of the prejudiced person's way of thinking about *anything*.

Allport describes the thinking of prejudiced individuals as bifurcated, or dichotomizing, and overly categorical. He explains that people who dichotomize in their mental operations tend to see important segments of reality entirely in terms of good versus bad, us versus them, in-group versus out-group. And he characterizes overly categorical thinking as "narrow-mindedness" and the "irrational dependence on rigid categories." Allport (1954, p. 78), commenting on the association between education and prejudice, writes: "Regarding education, it generally but not always appears from researches that people with college education are less intolerant [i.e., are less prejudiced] than people with grade school or high school education" (see also Adorno et al., 1950).

Other relatively early empirical research on status or "class" differences in intellectual functioning focuses explicitly on a variant of abstraction. For example, Findlay and McGuire (1957) find that middle-class children perform better on a test designed to measure "abstract behavior" than lower-class children, even with age, grade, and IQ held constant. Eells et al. (1951) examine the relationship between scores on both verbal and nonverbal intelligence tests and status factors and find the largest status differences on verbal material. They conclude that the "abstractness" of the items produces status differences in favor of middle-class respondents. Siller (1957), who conceives of abstraction as an aspect of conceptualization and conceptualization as a component of intelligence (a view that accords with the present study), also finds that high-status and low-status respondents (sixth graders) differ in abstraction performance, but he is skeptical about the substantive significance of the difference.

It is apparent from these relatively simple empirical studies that status differences are observed across even rather different conceptions of abstraction. This may indicate the existence of a robust and highly general underlying phenomenon. If there is truth to this, then we should be able to find supporting evidence elsewhere.

3.3. Constrained Belief Systems, Abstract Communication Styles, and Elaborated Speech Codes

Sociological research on belief systems, communication styles, and language use supports the findings discussed above and suggests some reasons why social class differences in intellectual functioning exist and how they evolve. Initially, it may appear that each of these topics is distantly, if at all, related to abstraction; however, further examination reveals a significant role for abstraction in each.

In a stimulating and influential study, Philip Converse (1964) relates social structural conditions (primarily differences in education) to degrees of constraint in belief systems. A belief system, says Converse, is "a configuration of ideas and attitudes in which the elements are bound together by some form of constraint" (p. 478). Constraint, in turn, is defined as the degree of *coherence* or *consistency* among attitudinal or ideational components. Although Converse assumes a rational approach to constraint, he does not specify what cognitive mechanics produce constraint. The concept of abstraction is useful for this purpose, for as we saw earlier, abstraction imposes constraint or structure on knowledge systems through the classification of ideas according to perceived similarities and differences. It will be remembered that similarities and differences are broadly defined here to include not merely surface level attributes and characteristics, but also likenesses and differences of function, time, place, and so forth.

Converse says that constrained belief systems are "remote," "generic," and composed of abstract, ideological principles. He contrasts constrained belief systems with the " 'limited horizons' . . . and 'concrete thinking' . . . of the ideational world of the poorly educated" (p. 483).[1] Although he explains that

[1]Note that whereas the level of constraint of a belief system is said to vary directly with the extent to which it is composed of "abstract principles," there is no *necessary* connection between these two characteristics. Indeed, confounding the two is parallel to not distinguishing between abstraction and abstractness—a distinction that we saw earlier, gets lost in the notion of abstract thinking. There are people who have neither great stores of information nor a mastery of abstract principles and yet their attitudinal constellations are highly constrained (i.e., consistent). The quality of constraint refers to the organization of thought rather than to its content.

level of constraint of belief systems in the general population is largely a function of education, Converse also recognizes that recurring combinations of idea-elements in belief systems derive from the configuration of interests and information tied to other niches in the social structure. He adopts a traditional sociology of knowledge approach by focusing on the connection between social position and political ideology but adds a cognitive psychological dimension with the concept of constraint, which assumes a cognitive mechanism that structures information, ideas, and beliefs. The limitations of this seminal work are that the nature of this constraint-producing cognitive mechanism is not elaborated and neither are the types of structural conditions, aside from education, which promote constraint. Further elaboration of the social conditioning of intellectual functioning is found in research on communication styles and language use, considered next.

Schatzman and Strauss (1955) use the abstract/concrete distinction to classify different styles of communication reflected in interview transcriptions of middle-class and lower-class respondents' descriptions of a local disaster caused by a tornado. They conclude that "in general, the thought and speech of middle-class persons is less concrete than that of the lower group."

> [The middle-class respondent] assumes multiple perspectives and communicates in terms of them. A variety of perspectives implies a variety of ways of ordering or framing detail. Moreover, he is able to classify and to relate to classes explicitly, which is but another way of saying that he is educated to assume multiple perspectives of rather wide scope [pp. 333, 336].

This overarching concern with classification subsumes abstraction as a means of categorization on the basis of similarities and differences. Schatzman and Strauss also argue that middle-class respondents' more frequent encounters with bureaucracies and sundry institutions facilitate their communication style, presumably by rewarding the more explicit verbal expression of one's circumstances, qualifications, attributes, needs, feelings, and so forth. This point of view contains the seeds of a more elaborate theory of language use developed by Basil Bernstein.

Bernstein's (1971–1973, inclusive) research on social class and language use contributes substantial detail to our understanding of how and why different locations in the structure of society facilitate or hinder cognitive processes underlying the outward expression of ideas and beliefs. Bernstein's conception of *speech codes* is central to his sociology of language. The speech code is the functional form of three principles of "verbal planning": *orientation* (which is akin to "selective attention" [cf. Neisser's (1967) "perceptual cycle"]), *association* (in the classic psychological sense), and *organization* (the overarching cognitive processes directly involved in generating meanings [cf. Sternberg's (1985) conception of metacognition]). Bernstein and his colleagues find that working-class children use a more *restricted* speech code, characterized by "meanings [that] are likely to be concrete, descriptive or narrative rather than analytic or abstract.'' The ways in which language is used by occupants of the lower social strata tends to be more context-dependent and linguistically implicit, meanings are more particularistic and ''tied to a local relationship and to a local social structure'' (Bernstein, 1971, pp. 175–176). On the other hand, ''the preparation and delivery of relatively explicit meaning is the major function of [the elaborated] code. This does not mean that these meanings are necessarily abstract, but abstraction inheres in the possibilities,'' writes Bernstein (p. 128).

Leaving aside the apparent confounding of abstraction with ''abstract meanings,'' let us focus on the different social conditions believed to support elaborated and restricted speech code use. First, it appears that restricted speech is more characteristic of lower-class children, whereas elaborated speech is more common among middle-class children. Bernstein maintains that restricted speech develops out of experience in a relatively homogeneous social structure in which interactive partners share many understandings and thus can take meanings for granted or communicate them implicitly through gesture, tone, slang, cliche, and vague reference. Because participants in homogeneous social settings interact primarily among themselves, much of their experience is shared with individuals like themselves. This places less demand on thought and language to make unique experience explicit and understood because there is less unique experience. In contrast, the social environments of middle-class children, both current and prospective, are more heterogeneous, which supports elaborate speech code use. Because Bernstein focuses on childhood, he emphasizes such socialization practices as the examples middle-class parents provide by giving their children detailed explanations and justifications for behaviors and expectations. Through such experiences children learn to adapt to the more heterogeneous, and as we shall see below, complex, social contexts they will face as adults.

On the side of theory, Bernstein provides an overarching psychological framework (even if the specific cognitive mechanics are largely unspecified), and he uses it to relate psychological outcomes to social structural dynamics. That is, his sociology of language does not rest with the observation of social class differences in speech code use; it depicts in some detail those aspects of experience—the proximate social conditions—in the higher and lower social strata that facilitate and hinder the development of verbal planning and speech code use. By extension this helps us to focus on social conditions that cultivate abstraction and that underlie the social class differences observed in the studies reviewed heretofore. It helps us to move from grand theories to middle-level theories and testable hypotheses (Merton, 1967).

On the empirical side, however, although the findings reported in Bernstein's three volumes of *Class, Codes, and Control* support his theory in general, they do not tell us much about the specific aspects of social class that matter most or about how their effects are transmitted. Moreover, the frequent practice of combining particular status variables (education, occupation, and family income) into a single index risks confounding different associations of these variables with outcome variables. We will have to look elsewhere for more sophisticated empirical research on the influence of specific aspects of socially stratified experience on intellectual functioning.

3.4. Work and Personality

In an extensive program of research spanning more than three decades, Melvin Kohn and Carmi Schooler (Kohn, 1977; Kohn & Schooler, 1983) have made important contributions to the understanding of social class differences in intellectual functioning and social values. Among the numerous aspects of personality they examine are: parental values and values for self (self-direction vs. conformity), self-conception (self-confidence, self-deprecation, anxiety, attribution of responsibility, and idea conformity), social orientation (authoritarian conservatism, criteria of morality, trustfulness, and stance toward change), and intellectual flexibility (perceptual flexibility and ideational flexibility). Not only are their measures of psychological functioning exceptionally rich, but they bring rigor and precision to the conceptualization and measurement of the structural components of social class.[2]

House (1981) argues, citing Kohn and Schooler's work as exemplary, that specification of the components of social structural conditions is a key feature of any theory that attempts to account for the effects of society on persons. In the following passage, Kohn and Schooler (1983, p. 21) explain their orientation:

> Interpreting the relationships of social stratification to values and orientations [and intellectual functioning] requires that we determine which of the many conditions of life associated with social stratification position actually contribute to explaining these relationships. . . . Primary among the conditions of life that vary continuously with education and occupational status are the occupational conditions conducive to or restrictive of the exercise of self-direction in work.

They observe that three aspects of occupational self-direction are pertinent to psychological functioning—the substantive complexity of work, closeness of supervision, and routinization of work—and through sophisticated analysis of data from a national sample of men, they find that occupational complexity is "clearly the most important of the three" (p. 64).

> By the substantive complexity of work we mean the degree to which the work, in its very substance, requires thought and independent judgment. Substantively complex work by its very nature requires making many decisions that must take into account ill-defined or apparently conflicting contingencies [p. 106].

They further analyze the conditions of substantively complex work into the complexity of work with things, data, and people (with an emphasis on the latter

[2]By now it should be clear that the use of the phrase social class, in Kohn's work, in Bernstein's, and here, is not identical to the Marxian definition of class as a function of workers' relationship to the means of production, to the product, and to ownership of capital used in production.

two) and the time spent in such activities. In their work with Karen Miller (Miller, Kohn, & Schooler, 1985, 1986), they have extended the conception of self-directed work to the realm of formal education. Educational self-direction requires "the use of initiative, thought, and judgment in schoolwork" (Miller, Kohn, & Schooler, 1985, p. 372), a conception that they say is clearly "directly analogous to the substantive complexity of work in paid employment" (p. 375).

For our purposes the most important findings from this research program are that job conditions influence intellectual functioning and values about oneself, one's children, and society and that psychological functioning, in turn, exercises its own (often lagged) effect on job conditions. In a remarkably broad and intensive program of research, the causal influence of work on intellectual functioning has been demonstrated "in countries of widely diverse cultures (United States, Japan, Poland), under a variety of different conditions (paid employment, school work, women's housework), and at different stages of the life span (students, younger workers, older workers)" (Schooler, 1989, p. 130). This would suggest the existence of a robust phenomenon underlying and explaining the linkages between environmental conditions and intellectual functioning.

3.5 The Theory of Psychological Effects of Complex Environments

Schooler (1984) marshals in additional evidence in support of the view that the dynamic linking job complexity and intellectual functioning is part of a more general process, broad enough to be called a theory of the psychological effects of complex environments. He explains that

> the complexity of an individual's environment is defined by its stimulus and demand characteristics. The more diverse the stimuli, the greater the number of decisions required, the greater the number of considerations to be taken into account in making these decisions, and the more ill-defined and apparently contradictory the contingencies, the more complex the environment. To the degree that the pattern of reinforcement within such an environment rewards cognitive effort, individuals should be motivated to develop their intellectual capacities and to generalize the resulting cognitive processes to other situations [p. 260].

Schooler builds on the findings that complex work experiences affect intellectual flexibility by citing supporting evidence from animal studies, psychological experiments, and sociological research. He concludes that "it is rare to find a theory, no matter how roughhewn, that is congruent with such a range of phenomena—one which stretches not only across populations, but across the research of academic disciplines from biochemistry to sociology" (p. 276).

Schooler's theory of psychological effects of complex environments provides the foundation for a much needed synthesis of research on the social determination of intellectual functioning across the life course. It, together with the fact that the level of environmental complexity and stimulation that parents provide their children is positively associated with familial socioeconomic status (see, e.g., Spaeth, 1976), helps to explain the social class differences in intellectual functioning reported in the literature reviewed earlier in this chapter. It embraces Schooler's (1972) finding that being raised in a complex and multifaceted childhood environment—as indicated by having a well educated father, a nondogmatic religion, living in an urban setting, and growing up in a region of the country far from the South—results in a higher level of adult intellectual functioning. It is consistent with research documenting more immediate effects of the quality and quantity of stimuli in family and preschool environments on psychological functioning in childhood (see references in Schooler, 1984). As for the effects of complex environments on intellectual functioning in old age, the theory is consistent with findings from longitudinal research supporting the view that "cognitive decline, like cognitive development, is conditioned to some extent on the nature and intensity of environmental stimulation" (Owens, 1966, p. 325; quoted in Schooler, 1984, p. 269). Willis and Schaie (1986), for example, report that cognitive decline observed in subjects in longitudinal studies can be reversed through intervention training programs that increase the complexity of subjects' environments by providing sources of intellectual stimulation.

Schaie (1983) also puts much emphasis on sources of environmental complexity as the cognitive stimulation that helps maintain intellectual functioning into old age. Observing that there are "vast individual differences in intellectual change across adulthood . . . ranging from early decrement for some persons to maintenance of function into very advanced age for others," Schaie adopts the following orientation to explain these differences:

> It is clear that a favorable environment as characterized by an advantaged SES is related not only to high levels of intellectual functioning, but also to the maintenance of such functioning into later life. The mechanism involved here is likely to be the maintenance of varied opportunities for environmental stimulation. I find myself concluding that the use-it-or-lose-it principle applies not only to the maintenance of muscular flexibility, but to the maintenance of flexible life styles and a related high level of intellectual performance as well [pp. 128-129].[3]

Schaie and Willis (1986), Arbuckle et al. (1986), and others similarly conclude from empirical results that "high levels of environmental stimulation" and an "engaged lifestyle" help to maintain intellectual functioning in old age.

---

[3]Richard Nisbitt has observed that the metaphor of the mind as a muscle that becomes stronger with practice "contradicts what most 20th century cognitive psychologists have believed. . . . In the early 1900s, many psychologists rejected the classic notion that the brain was a muscle that could be trained with memorization, Latin grammar and problems in logic" (The Ann Arbor News, 1987). Nisbett's own research supports the metaphor. For example, he found that students who were taught inferential abstract rule systems could later apply these "abstract studies" in answering questions designed for the experiment.

3.5.1. A Recurring Theme

The idea that complex and differentiated physical and social environments are conducive to intellectual development first arose in this book in the previous chapter's discussion of cognitive development in childhood. As children grow older they are exposed to more complex environments and this stimulates intellectual development. The same idea appears again in this chapter in the discussion of status differences in intellectual functioning. Higher positions on status dimensions are associated with more complex environments and this in turn stimulates more complex intellectual functioning. Next we turn to a third topical area in which this idea is current, namely, the study of the effects of modernization processes on individuals.

3.6. Societal Development and Individual Modernity

Alex Inkeles' (Inkeles, 1983; Inkeles & Smith, 1974) investigation of the individual-level effects of modernization provides another vantage point for examining the relationship between environmental and cognitive complexity. The processes that epitomize modernization—mass education, urbanization, industrialization, bureaucratization, and rapid communication and transportation—produce increasingly differentiated, specialized, complex social milieu, and thus the proximate conditions of social experience that are conducive to the development of intellectual skills. Using cross-national data, Inkeles examines covariation between institutional and social arrangements that vary by modernity level and syndromes of traditional and modern personality characteristics.

Inkeles' research program, like Kohn and Schooler's, is multifaceted and rich with detail. Here we focus only on the cognitive aspects of his scale of "overall modernity"—a multidimensional index of psychological orientations and operations. Although the intellectual facets of individual modernity are never specified in much detail, it is said that they include the familiar notions of a mind that "does not insist on excessively premature closure" and is "tolerant of diversity," "cognitively flexible," and "field independent."[4] Inkeles argues that these intellectual orientations are learned through exposure to modern institutional arrangements. Here, as in Kohn and Schooler's research, school and work tend to be the most important contexts for becoming modern or gaining intellectual flexibility. Inkeles (1983, p. 20) explains:

> Following the leads Marx provided when he declared that one's relationship to the mode of production shapes one's consciousness, we may expect individuals to learn to be modern by incorporating within themselves principles which are embedded in the organizational practices of the institutions in which they live and work. . . . Individual modernity then becomes a quality learned by the incorporation into the self-system of certain

[4]Cognitive flexibility and field independence are also basic to Kohn and Schooler's conception of intellectual flexibility and can be traced to a research program reported in Witkin et al. (1962) and discussed in the final chapter of this book.

qualities characteristic of particular institutional environments . . . [e.g.,] common principles of organization, procedures for assigning power and prestige, modes for allocating rewards and punishment, and approaches to the management of time.

Additional evidence that social change affects mental processes—and more specifically, that complex environments foster the development of cognitive complexity—is from a unique field experiment conducted by the Soviet psychologist A.R. Luria (1976). During the 1930s Luria interviewed people living in the Central Asian steppes, where several villages were being radically restructured in order to reduce illiteracy and to diminish the influence of Islam. Luria believed that by conducting research early "during a period of rapid and fundamental reorganization of social structures" he would "observe the sociohistorical shaping of mental processes," because, as he puts it, the very "structure of mental activity—not just the specific content but also the general forms basic to all cognitive processes—changes in the course of historical development" (1976, pp. 8, 12).

Luria's subjects were divided into three groups according to their exposure to social change: illiterate peasants from remote villages, collective farm laborers with a minimal amount of schooling, and those who had as much as 1 or 2 years of schooling. From intensive interviews with people in all three groups (people, it is important to note, for whom membership was not voluntary), Luria drew the following conclusions.

> The facts show convincingly that the structure of cognitive activity does not remain static during different stages of historical development and that the most important forms of cognitive processes—perception, generalization, deduction, reasoning, imagination, and analysis of one's own inner life—vary as the conditions of social life change and the rudiments of knowledge are mastered [p. 161].

Luria had a special interest in abstraction. He reasoned that "once people acquire education, they make increasingly greater use of categorization to express ideas that objectively reflect reality" (p. 99). And he explained that the concrete thinking of his subjects

> is neither innate nor genetically determined. It results from illiteracy and the rudimentary types of activity that have prevailed in these subjects' daily experience. When the pattern of their lives changes and the range of their experience broadens, when they learn to read and write, to become part of a more advanced culture, the greater complexity of their activity stimulates new ideas. These changes, in turn bring about a radical reorganization of their habits of thinking, so they learn to use and appreciate the value of theoretical procedures that formerly seemed irrelevant [p. 79].

Luria's research clearly shows that environmental complexity discourages concrete thinking and supports the development of abstraction and other reflective modes of thought.

3.6.1. The Theme Again

Viewed from three different research angles, environmental complexity is seen as an important determinant of intellectual functioning. Complex environments provide sources of stimulation that are necessary for the biologically maturing child to progress through stages of cognitive development. Complex environments teach students and workers to be self-directed and intellectually flexible and they help elders to maintain youthful levels of intellectual functioning. Complex environments account for differences in intellectual functioning among children, between social classes, and across levels of modernity. Probably the source of environmental complexity that has received the most attention is education, followed closely by occupational experience. Of course parents and the family environment are important sources of environmental complexity for children.

A variety of cognitive outcomes are related to experience in complex environments. These include specific modes of thinking such as prejudice and ethnocentrism, and more general orientations such as communication style, language use, constrained beliefs, intellectual flexibility, and individual modernity. This recurring theme—that complex environments foster cognitive complexity—appears in yet another, fourth, context, but this time with specific reference to abstraction. This is the topic of the following section, which examines ideas from the sociology of knowledge bearing on the relationship between environmental and cognitive complexity. This literature adds a perspective that not only extends the way we think about environmental complexity but increases the range of possible indicators of it.

3.7. The Sociology of Knowledge

"*The basic literature* of the sociology of knowledge is widely considered useless as a source of guidance for empirical work, especially for research in a quantitative vein," writes Werner Landecker (1982, p. 73) in a highly integrative essay on the use of survey research in the sociology of knowledge. Landecker argues that this attitude is due, in part, to the widely held but "very restrictive conception of the traditional pursuits" of this area as limited to "the intellectual products of experts," "the intellectual elite," and "the esoteric doctrines of the few" (p. 74). Landecker's own view is that "a variety of basic problems in [the sociology of knowledge] are not limited to the elite level but involve variables on which everybody can get a score, although not necessarily a high score" (p. 74). Research in the sociology of knowledge "is primarily concerned with the impact of sociostructural factors on variable properties of cognitive ideas," he says.

It is in this context that Landecker sets out the definition of abstraction adopted in this book—as a mode of thought flanked by concrete thinking on one side and by stereotype thinking on the other and distinguished from both. He brings together some incipient ideas about its social determination from the writings of Simmel and Mannheim and elaborates them into an insightful hypothesis about the effect of structural overlap on abstraction. As we consider the development of this hypothesis and the meaning and significance of its key concept, structural overlap, it is interesting to see that, in its original formulation, it was based on a concern with the psychological effects of modernization.

Both Georg Simmel (1955) and Karl Mannheim (1936) observe that the processes of urbanization and industrialization are characterized, in part, by the transition from social groups which are relatively homogeneous in their composition to increasingly interconnected, overlapping, and heterogenous social groups. They realize that as societies modernize there is an attendant increase in "the association of persons who share a basis for interaction and their mutual relationship itself but who also differ with regard to their membership in other groups" (Lee & Landecker, 1989, p. 3). Each gives special attention to the structural qualities of the resulting social arrangements: Simmel speaks of the "intersection of social circles" and Mannheim discusses "social circulation," groups "merging into one another," and "processes of group contact and interpenetration." Mannheim (1936, p. 8) writes that, as a result of increased social circulation, "[f]orms of thought and experience, which had hitherto developed independently, enter into one and the same consciousness."

In his rather boldly stated "theory of the social genesis of abstraction," Mannheim expressly links the development of abstraction to participation in merging social groups. He argues that "[t]he trend towards a higher stage of abstraction is a correlate of the amalgamation of social groups" (p. 302). Before Mannheim, Simmel (1955, pp. 127-128) spoke more cautiously of an "analogue" between abstraction[5] and "the association of homogeneous members from heterogeneous groups," or "the association of like individuals, who are otherwise affiliated with quite alien and unrelated groups."

Landecker (1982; Lee & Landecker, 1989) builds on the work of Simmel and Mannheim by broadening the focus on group membership to include other structural units of a collectivity, such as social strata, thereby replacing Simmel's notion of intersecting social circles with his own concept of structural overlap.

> In a structurally differentiated population, structural overlap exists to the extent that different structural units coincide in their membership, or that a third unit contains members of two others, or that members move from one unit to another [Landecker, 1982, p. 79].

The concept of structural overlap also allows Landecker to shift attention from the social structural shaping of forms of thought at different time periods (the specific concern of Simmel and Mannheim) to the differential social structural shaping of thought across individuals at a single point in time.[6]

In the following passage Landecker (1982, pp. 80–81) makes the causal connection between structural overlap and abstraction explicit:

---

[5]Although Mannheim actually used the term abstraction, Simmel (1955, p. 127) merely implied it when he spoke of a mode of thought in which "a higher concept binds together the elements which a great number of very different perceptual complexes have in common."

[6]Elsewhere (Lee & Landecker, 1989, p. 5) we argue that "[s]ince the frequency of structural overlap as an object of personal experience varies not only among different stages in the development of a sociey but also among different persons at the same time, one should be able to observe its effect on abstraction not only by diachronic comparisons but also by synchronic comparisons in a cross-section of the same population."

The hypothesis linking abstraction to structural overlap rests largely on a certain parallelism, if not isomorphism, between both. The distinction between shared and discrepant properties characterizes not only the process of abstraction but also the social experience produced by structural overlap. If, for example, structural units A and B overlap with C, all persons in the area of overlap share their C connection with one another but differ in their A and B connections; all As share their A connection, but only those in the area of overlap are also Cs. Thus, in groups marked by structural overlap, shared and discrepant affiliations are intermingled and yet distinct. . . .

Durkheim and Mauss (1963, pp. 32, 82), as well as Scheler (1960, p. 58), have argued that group properties tend to function as thought models—that the patterns of group structure that people experience are reflected in their thought patterns. When applied to structural overlap, this theory suggests that the experienced convergence, but not fusion, of shared and of discrepant affiliations will foster a tendency to distinguish between shared and discrepant properties—that is, to make abstractions—not only in the context of that structural experience itself but also in other situations. The same tendency should find support in the fact that structural overlap produces occasions for comparing behavior patterns that serve the same function—for example, to express anger or to display status—but that also differ in certain properties because the observed actors represent different groups or strata.

It is assumed that structural overlap functions as a "thought model" for abstraction.[7] The thought model concept is part of what Wuthnow (1987, pp. 303-304) calls the "correspondence theory of knowledge." Drawing on the work of Mary Douglas (1970), Wuthnow argues that a determinate relation exists between social conditions and symbols (i.e., knowledge, ideology)—and, we may add, forms of thought—when "the intrinsic structure or form of the two is so naturally similar that virtually anyone can recognize the correspondence."

Similar hypotheses have been derived from sociological theories that relate experience in multiple role settings to positive developmental outcomes. Urie Bronfenbrenner (1979) hypothesizes that "development is enhanced as a direct function of the number of structurally different settings in which the developing person participates." The idea of "structurally different settings" is closely related to the concept of structural overlap: "The positive developmental effect of participation in multiple settings occur in cultural or subcultural contexts that are different from each other, in terms of ethnicity, social class, religion, age group, or other background factors" (p. 213). Bronfenbrenner notes that this hypothesis reflects Lewin's (1935) emphasis "on a close interconnection and isomorphism between the structure of the person and of the situation."

[7]This assumption "elaborates the simple statement of a relationship by adding what Merton (1949, pp. 254–258), in his analysis of Mannheim's work, describes as a 'connective,' i.e., that property or function of a structural factor which accounts for its hypothesized effect, thus providing a rationale for the hypothesis itself" (Lee & Landecker, 1989). As discussed later, the thought model in Kohn and Schooler's work is the process of learning–generalization; in Inkeles' work it is the closely related process of social learning.

Rose Coser (1975) makes parallel observations in an essay whose title, "Complexity of Roles as a Seedbed of Individual Autonomy," summarizes the issue as well as any 9 or 10 words could. Coser is explicit about the positive effects of experience in complex and overlapping social environments. She observes that whereas the *plurality* or *segmentation* of social roles has often been seen as a source of alienation and disintegration of the self-system, the opposite view is expressed by Simmel, "who sees in such segmentation a structural basis for modern individualism" (p. 241).

Clearly these parallels between and among Bronfenbrenner's and Coser's ideas, Landecker's structural overlap hypothesis, and the modernity literature discussed earlier are significant. It must be stressed, however, that a unique aspect of Landecker's approach is that because the mode of cognitive functioning is quite explicitly identified, it is thus possible to consider equally specific hypotheses. We turn to these next.

3.8. The Structural Overlap Hypothesis

A number of empirically testable hypotheses can be derived from the thesis that the experience of structural overlap provides the opportunity for perceiving similarities and differences among homogeneous social actors who participate in heterogeneous social groups; in other words, that structural overlap fosters abstraction. They can be derived simply by elaborating the types of structural overlap that are experienced to varying degrees in a structurally differentiated population.

Status inconsistency is a type of structural overlap in which an individual occupies different vertical positions on two structural dimensions. A black physician, a female chief executive officer, and an unemployed PhD have inconsistent statuses. The structural overlap hypothesis suggests that status inconsistency should be positively related to abstraction (*ceteris paribus*) because it affords a vantage point from which the observer can discern differences between members of the respective status groups while also seeing what they have in common. *Occupational mobility*, personal or intergenerational, is another form of structural overlap. Whether an individual changes occupational statuses or one's father's occupational status differs from one's own, either way this structural condition has the potential for fostering abstraction for the same reasons given for status inconsistency. Structural characteristics of the *family of origin* may also overlap: one or both parents may be from another country, or parents may combine different ethnic, religious, or educational backgrounds. These conditions provide numerous opportunities to observe similarities and differences in the same dyad.

The union of separate biographies in *marriage* is a potential wellspring of opportunities for observing differences and similarities. For example, when a Jew and a Gentile marry, when a black marries a white, when one spouse comes from a wealthy family and the other comes from a poor family, then not only is it a pretty good bet that they have discovered important similarities along with their obvious differences, but it is just as certain that they will continue to do so as long as they stay together. The *friendship network* is another source of structural overlap. The more diverse the network of friends, the greater the opportunity to observe what one has in common with people who are older or younger, richer or poorer, more or less educated, who have a higher or lower occupational status, or who observe a different religion than oneself. Finally, because racial statuses coincide in *racially mixed neighborhoods*, this too is a form of structural overlap that is predicted to foster abstraction. Each of these hypotheses will be tested in the following chapter.

3.9. A Note on the Link Between Complex Environments and Intellectual Functioning

Kohn and Schooler assume that the process of learning-generalization—"learning from the job and generalizing what has been learned to other realms of life" (Miller, Slomczynski, & Kohn, 1985, p. 593)—accounts for the impact of work conditions on intellectual flexibility as well as other aspects of adult personality and activity. Similarly, Inkeles (1983, p. 20) maintains that of the five most likely explanations of variation in levels of individual modernity—innate disposition, early family milieu, shared culture, diffusion-imitation-dependency, and social learning—"the social learning theory would account for by far the greater proportion of variance explained." Likewise, Schooler's encompassing theory of the psychological effects of complex environments is based on a parallel learning model; namely, that stimulus and demand characteristics of environments, and their reinforcement schedules, determine levels of cognitive effort and flexibility required for adaptation.

It is interesting to find that all of these authors acknowledge limits on how well these linking processes are understood. For example, even if Kohn and Schooler's research demonstrates a causal connection between doing substantively complex work and increased intellectual flexibility, and even if this finding is extremely robust, holding up across cultures, under different conditions of work, and at different times in the life course, Schooler (1989, p. 130) nevertheless observes that "we have isolated neither the specific characteristics of the environment nor the exact cognitive mechanisms through which this process takes place." In a similar vein, Inkeles (1983, p. 20) says that "we have far to go in understanding precisely which features of schools and factories make them effective teachers of modernity, and how such features achieve their results."

Assuming that social learning theory and the learning-generalization model explain a substantial part of the effect of environmental complexity on intellectual functioning, the question remains how to identify with greater precision the environmental conditions and cognitive mechanisms involved. It is worth considering that the degree to which causes or stimuli emanating from the environment can be specified *can be no greater than* the degree to which any psychological effect or mode of cognitive functioning is specified. This proposition gains some support in the present study, where abstraction has been specified in considerable detail and where it has been possible to focus rather explicitly on a number of features of complex environments that are conducive to its development and maintenance across the life course. In broad terms, the environmental conditions that facilitate the development of abstraction provide opportunities to learn what ostensibly different objects of perception have in common. Such opportunities, which are elaborated in the next chapter in the form of hypotheses, are more prevalent in self-directed educational and occupational activities, and in middle-class socialization practices and family environments. In addition to these sources of cognitive stimulation,-it is also anticipated that overlapping structural configurations of statuses and social groups provide opportunities for the development of abstraction.

3.10. Chapter Summary

This chapter addresses three broad concerns. First, it relates abstraction to several psychological variables with sociological relevance: ethnocentrism, prejudice, Converse's notion of constrained belief systems, Bernstein's elaborated and restricted speech codes, Kohn and Schooler's intellectual flexibility, and Inkeles' individual modernity. Second, it examines various sources of environmental stimulation—from the family milieu and parent's socialization practices, to conditions of educational and occupational activity, to large scale processes of urbanization and industrialization—which have important psychological effects. And third, it reflects on the processes that link environmental conditions to intellectual functioning.

This tripartite endeavor has a parallel in what House (1977) and others call the three faces of social psychology. House argues that a genuinely multidisciplinary approach to a social psychological topic must: (a) describe the individual level outcome(s) of interest in a psychologically sophisticated manner, (b) specify the relevant components of the macrosocial causes or conditions of the psychological outcome, and (c) elaborate the proximate social conditions and processes that link macrosocial conditions to psychological outcomes. It has taken all of three chapters to respond to this threefold challenge. Now it is time to bring data to bear, wherever possible, on the ideas discussed heretofore.

4
Empirical Findings

4.1. Introduction

This chapter brings concerns from the three preceding ones together in the analysis of sample survey data. The first chapter laid the foundation for empirical work by specifying definitions of abstraction, by conceptually clarifying it, and by discussing its educational, occupational, and everyday uses. The second chapter focused on several important methodological issues that arise in the study of the development of abstraction across the life course. It was concluded that cross-sectional studies of adult intellectual development such as the present one must take measures to reduce, if not remove, the spurious contribution of birth cohort differences in social experiences to the appearance of intellectual decline with age. The third chapter reflected on a number of possible socioenvironmental determinants of abstraction, which vary across cohorts as well as status positions and social structural locations, in the context of Schooler's (1987) theory of psychological effects of complex environments.

The next few sections introduce and describe a measure of abstraction which (a) incorporates both the nonconcrete and the nonstereotype dimensions, (b) is suitable for sample survey research, and (c) shares coding guidelines with some of the most widely used clinical measures of the detection of commonalities. Then three analysis sections follow. The first analysis estimates the relationship between age and abstraction net of cohort-related differences in major sources of environmental complexity at different stages in the life course. The second analysis focuses on older respondents, again examining relations among age, environmental complexity, and abstraction, but in this case the sources of environmental complexity considered are particularly relevant to the later period of life. The third analysis tests several forms of the structural overlap hypothesis proposed by Landecker (1982) and discussed in the last chapter. Finally, the concluding section summarizes the findings from these analyses.

4.2. Measuring Abstraction

The various measures of abstraction discussed in chapter 1 are not ideal for survey research purposes since they were designed for use with psychiatric patients, students, and subjects in psychology experiments; that is, with people who expect to be tested. Survey research, on the other hand, collects information from randomly selected respondents in situations where there are few formal role expectations and constraints. Thus, there is little to prevent respondents from refusing to do an interview, from declining to answer certain questions, or from prematurely ending an interview they regard as boring, threatening, or intrusive. If the study of cognitive functioning is to benefit from the increased representation, external validity, and realism of survey research (cf. Kish, 1987), then questionnaire items—whether they measure abstraction or attitudes, objective behavior or subjective states—must be clear and straightforward. These goals are more nearly achieved by crafting questions using *simple language* and *common concepts,* questions presenting *manageable tasks,* and questions based on *widespread information* (Converse & Presser, 1986, pp. 10–31).

As part of his effort to show that sociology of knowledge concepts and hypotheses are amenable to survey research, Landecker (1981, pp. 75–76) provides several useful prescriptions for writing cognitively oriented survey questions. First, he says, shun questions like "Of the five things below, four are alike in a certain way. Which one is not like these four?" because they make the respondent feel that he or she is being tested. Second, write questions with topical appeal, thereby reducing the likelihood that respondents will experience questions as being irrelevant and thus will not be motivated to respond to them seriously. And third, make the lowest possible demands on information by writing "questions that are meaningful to the poorly educated but . . . [that] are not meaningless to the well educated" (p. 76).

The fact that none of the measures of abstraction considered earlier explicitly incorporates indicators of the nonstereotype dimension of the concept also precludes their use here. For the purpose of measuring the tendency to use abstraction across a wide range of individuals randomly selected from a large metropolitan area, a number of survey questions were written in a manner that is consistent with the above guidelines. After pretesting these questions, the principal investigators and staff of the 1980 Detroit Area Study of the University of Michigan decided that three items would be used to indicate the nonconcrete dimension and two items would be used to indicate the nonstereotype dimension.

4.2.1. The Nonconcrete Dimension

Each indicator of nonconcrete thinking asks whether two familiar objects (students, neighborhoods, institutions) have *anything* in common or whether they are *entirely* different.

1. Let's talk about two high school students. One studies very little, but spends long hours in the gym and has won several contests in gymnastics. The other studies hard and gets good grades, but has no interest in sports. Do these two people seem *entirely different* or do they seem to have *something in common?*

2. Now I would like you to think of two different kinds of communities, wealthy and not wealthy—say, Grosse Pointe and Highland Park. Do you think there are any important similarities between people who live in wealthy areas and people who live in less wealthy areas? (Are people in Grosse Pointe similar to people in Highland Park in any important ways?)

3. Do you think a school has *something in common* with a hospital or are they *totally different?*

A response stating that there are no important similarities, that the two objects in question are entirely or totally different, or one in which an alleged similarity is actually a statement of differences, is scored at the lowest, concrete level. Stated commonalities are evaluated as being at the highest, nonconcrete level or at the intermediate level. The criteria used to derive these judgements are discussed below in section 4.3.

Table 4.1 presents the distribution of respondents (n = 615) across the three response categories for each of the three nonconcrete questions. Clearly there is substantial variation to be explained. Also note, by comparing the left and right columns of figures, that whereas there is nearly an equal percentage of nonconcrete and concrete responses to the scholar/athlete question, each successive question "loses" an additional 10% of cases from the nonconcrete category to the concrete category. This suggests that abstraction becomes more difficult as subject matter increases in abstractness (i.e., generality), as it does in this case from *students* to *neighborhoods* to *institutions*.

4.2.2. The Nonstereotype Dimension

Nonstereotype thinking is operationally defined as recognizing important differences among things that are nevertheless viewed as alike. Respondents were asked whether they agree, strongly agree, disagree, strongly disagree, or neither agree nor disagree with the following statements:

1. There are two kinds of countries in the world: those that are democratic and those that are not.

2. There are a few exceptions, but in general, immigrants who come from the same country are pretty much alike.

TABLE 4.1 Distribution of responses to the questions used to measure the nonconcrete dimension of abstraction (n = 615)

	Nonconcrete (%)	Intermediate (%)	Concrete (%)
Scholar/athlete	43	17	40
Two communities	32	15	53
School/hospital	22	15	63

TABLE 4.2 Distribution of responses to the questions used to measure the nonstereotype dimension of abstraction (n = 615)

	Stereotypic			Nonstereotypic	
	Strongly Agree (%)	Agree (%)	Don't know/ Depends (%)	Disagree (%)	Strongly Disagree (%)
Two kinds of countries	3.7	58.0	5.0	29.1	4.1
All immigrants are alike	4.1	56.1	3.3	32.7	3.9

The first item is based on indicators of "stereotypy" from Adorno et al.'s (1950) F Scale and the second item is based on Levinson and Sanford's (1944) Anti-Semitism Scale. The distribution of respondents across response categories is presented in Table 4.2. Strong agreement receives a score of 1, neutrality a score of 3, and strong disagreement a score of 5.

4.2.3. An Abstraction Index

Unless there are theoretical reasons to suggest otherwise (as, e.g., in section 4.7.1.), the two dimensions of abstraction will be used as joint indicators of a single construct. The conceptual work of chapter 1 argues that abstraction is a function of both nonconcrete thinking (seeing similarities among distinct items) and nonstereotype thinking (seeing differences among similar items). This measurement model can be tested using the confirmatory factor analysis features of LISREL (Joreskog, 1988). Table 4.3 presents estimates of the goodness of fit of a one-factor model based on the view that the five questions indicate a single construct with no multidimensionality, and a two-factor model based on the view that these questions measure two distinct constructs that may or may not themselves comprise a single higher order construct. The fact that the chi-square statistic for the two-factor model is *not* significant but that it *is* significant for the one-factor model suggests that the five questions do indeed measure two distinct modes of thought. But in addition, the fact that the two factors correlate between themselves at .57 supports the assumption that abstraction, as conceived of here, is reflected in their shared variance.[1] Therefore, the five questions are combined into an additive index in which each nonconcrete item contributes from one to three points and each nonstereotype item contributes one to five points. This abstraction index ranges from a low score of 5 to a high score of 19, and 67% of all cases are within 2.85 points above and below the mean of 11.0. The alpha coefficient of reliability is .53.

[1]A second-stage factor analysis is not possible because too few questions are available.

[2]Other scaling alternatives were tried, but in comparison with the additive version their associations with criterion variables (age, respondent's education, and occupational complexity) were lower (see Lee, 1988, chap. 1).

TABLE 4.3 Standardized loadings of maximum likelihood confirmatory factor analysis

	One-Factor Model	Two-Factor Model	
	Factor 1	Factor 1	Factor 2
School/athlete	.526	.572	
School/hospital	.545	.601	
Two communities	.513	.558	
Two kinds of countries	.496		.630
All Immigrants are alike	.480		.598
Chi-square	21.15	.93	
	(p = .001)	(p = .921)	
	df = 5	df = 4	

Note: Estimates were computed with LISREL. VII using a polychoric correlation matrix computed with PRELIS.

4.3. Coding Similarities Items

Of all the measures of abstraction listed in the compendium in chapter 1, the Verbal Relations Test from the Stanford-Binet Intelligence Scale and the Similarities Test from the Wechsler Intelligence Scales come the closest to being suitable for use in survey research. Like the nonconcrete questions described above, many of the questions included in these tests are straightforward, use simple concepts, make relatively little demand on vocabulary knowledge, and require little more than the detection of commonalities (in other words, they are unidimensional). Unfortunately, copyright restrictions prevent the easy incorporation of questions from these tests into survey research questionnaires. Nevertheless, these tests' scoring criteria are useful for our purposes because they were developed on the basis of considerable experience with questions that solicit the recognition of similarities among otherwise distinct objects of analysis.

The Verbal Relations Test consists of 18 questions, each of which presents four items in the form *a, b, c, NOT d.* The instructions are as follows:

> In each of the following questions four things are listed. The first three things are alike and they differ from the fourth thing. For each question tell how the first three things are alike but different from the fourth.
>
> Example: Coffee, tea, apple juice, NOT cake
>
> Response: *You can drink the first three but you cannot drink cake.*

There are rather terse guidelines for scoring responses either "pass" or "fail" in the *Guide for Administering and Scoring the Fourth Edition* of the Stanford-Binet Intelligence Scale (Thorndike, Hagen, Sattler, 1986, p. 135):

> To receive credit on the Verbal Relations Test, a response must state what is similar about the first three things that is *not* true of the fourth thing. The examinee must focus on the essential similarity among the first three things that is not true for the fourth thing.

One must deduce what an "essential similarity" is from the examples in the *Guide* of pass, fail, and "queried" responses.

The Similarities Test has more explicit and detailed scoring criteria. Each of the 14 Similarities questions on the WAIS-R and the 17 questions on the WISC-R presents two items and asks how they are alike (examples are: a *candle* and a *lamp,* an *apple* and a *banana, anger* and *joy,* an *egg* and a *seed*). All items are scored 2 (high), 1, or 0 (except for the first four, simplest items on the WISC-R, which are scored 1 or 0). The scoring criteria provided in the WAIS-R manual (Wechsler, 1981) and the WISC-R manual (Wechsler, 1974) are identical: it is said that scoring is based on (a) "the degree of understanding expressed" and (b) "the quality of the response" (1981, p. 134). *Degree of understanding* simply means whether or not the subject actually "abstract[s] something similar about the members of the pair."

> Some subjects are unable to do this and may respond to each member separately rather than to the pair as a whole ("You see with your eyes and hear with your ears"). Although such a response is a true statement, it is scored 0 since it tells how the members of the pair are dissimilar rather than how they are similar [p. 134].

Judging the *quality of the response* is necessary only when a similarity is stated. Again, according to Wechsler:

> The degree of abstraction of the subject's response is an important determinant of the score. That is why pertinent general categorizations are given 2 points, while the naming of one or more common properties or functions of the members of the pair (a more concrete problem-solving approach) merits only 1 point [p. 134].

The crucial idea here is "pertinent general categorizations." All perceived similarities are categorizations but if they are too specific, or concrete, then they do not satisfy the condition of generality. On the other hand, if they are too general, or overinclusive, then they do not satisfy the condition of pertinence. Wechsler does not make these distinctions explicit but merely implies them when he explains:

> [S]tating that a dog and a lion (item 2) are "Animals" (their general category) earns a higher score than saying "They both have tails" (a property common to each). On the other hand, stating that an orange and a banana (item 1) are "Fruit" earns more credit than stating that both are "Foods"; while the category of "fruit" is less general than that of "food," it is the more pertinent category [p. 134].

In short then, two guidelines are used for coding Similarities items. First, if no similarity is recognized, the response is simply coded 0. If a similarity is stated, the highest score (2) is given to a response that is general (that is, at a high level of abstractness) without being overinclusive (that is, not pertinent). And when a stated similarity is either not general enough or is too general, an intermediate score of 1 is given.

Responses to the three nonconcrete questions can be coded using the same guidelines. If it is said that the two objects in question are entirely different or have no important similarities, this response is scored at the lowest level. Statements of differences, such as "Schools educate and hospitals help the sick" and

"They are richer in Grosse Pointe," and statements of functional relationships, such as "You have to go to school to work in a hospital," are also scored at the lowest level. Similarities that are either overinclusive (not pertinent or essential) or at a low level of generality are scored at the intermediate level. Examples of overinclusive responses are: for the scholar/athlete question, "They are both high school students" and "Both are people"; for the neighborhoods question, "All are human beings" and "All live near Detroit." For the school/hospital question, an example of a similarity at a low level of abstractness is "Both have many rooms." Examples of similarities coded at the highest level, which are neither overinclusive nor too specific, are: for the scholar/athlete question, "They both have goals" and "Both work hard"; for the school/hospital question, "They both help people" and "Both are institutions"; and for the neighborhoods question, "Both have the same basic needs," "Both pay taxes and obey laws," and "Both have good people and bad people."

4.4. The Sample

The data analyzed in this study were collected between April and July of 1980 by the Detroit Area Study, a research and training facility of the University of Michigan. The sample was selected using multistage area probability sampling from a population frame of about 4.2 million people living in 1.4 million dwelling units located in the three-county region of southeastern Michigan (which includes the city of Detroit). Information was obtained from 615 respondents aged 18 to 88 years. To ensure population representation and efficiency of interviewing, census tracts were stratified by several socioeconomic indicators at the first stage of selection. At every stage of selection a systematic probability proportional to size design was employed. The response rate was 78.4%.

4.5. Environmental Complexity from Status-Related Sources

Turning back to Figure 2.1, in which the negative relationship between age and abstraction is displayed, let us now ask to what extent this fairly precipitous downward slope is moderated once differences in exposure to environmental complexity are statistically controlled. We shall also consider which of the status-related sources of complexity considered here—childhood environment, years of educational attainment, occupational complexity, and labor force participation—have important effects of their own on abstraction. Furthermore, what are the significant indirect paths through which age and these status-related sources of environmental complexity influence abstraction?

4.5.1. Hypotheses

Although some may believe the conditions of childhood are all important determinants of personality characteristics in adulthood, from the life course point of view environmental conditioning and social learning are lifelong processes. Thus, whereas it is hypothesized that early experience in complex physical and social environments has a lasting effect on abstraction in adulthood, it is also readily recognized that exposure to complex environments facilitates transitions into similarly complex educational, occupational, and postretirement environments, which are expected to have their own effects on abstraction.

Two general sources of intellectual stimulation for children are (a) exposure to physical environments which, by design or happenstance, serve instructional ends, and (b) engagement in mentoring relationships with parents, older siblings, relatives, teachers, and/or others. Complex physical environments provide ready access to instructional toys, games, and televisions programs, to books and magazines, and to such technical/scientific equipment as computers, calculators, telescopes, and so forth. Complex social environments are created by mentors who interact with a child on a slightly advanced intellectual level. There are many ways in which this is done: by reading together, going to museums and zoos and on other educational outings, using elaborated speech to give explicit and rational explanations, and valuing and encouraging at least partly intellectual rather than purely emotive responses. Of course these sources of complexity are usually combined, as for example when a family takes a vacation that broadens their exposure to diversity of place, people, and things. On the other hand, it also stands to reason that recurrent exposure to monotonous and relatively homogeneous physical and interpersonal environments during childhood hinders intellectual development and that this is likely to be reflected in lower abstraction performance in adulthood.

If the data support a positive relationship between complexity of childhood environments and abstraction, and if older adults were exposed to less environmental complexity as children, then this would help to moderate or explain some of the age-related decline in abstraction. Moreover, as noted more generally above, whereas exposure to complex environments in youth should have a direct positive impact on abstraction in adulthood, it should also have indirect effects via educational and occupational experiences.

Of all the sources of environmental complexity that might be expected to have a direct effect on abstraction performance in adulthood, educational experience stands out as probably the most important. Already we have reflected on types of educational activity that appear to provide direct instruction in abstraction (see chapter 1). Thus, there are good reasons to believe that the lower educational attainment of earlier birth cohorts accounts for a portion of the age-related decline in abstraction. The impact of education on abstraction is also likely to reflect, indirectly, the influence of one's upbringing, for it is known that parental expectations are an important determinant of children's academic achievements (Seginer, 1983).

In addition to having a positive, direct effect, higher educational attainment should also foster abstraction through its association with occupational complexity. Generally speaking, the higher one's education, the more complex their occupation, and the more complex the occupation, the greater the demand on abstraction skills. This can be illustrated with respect to two occupations that many regard as among the most complex, namely, the practice of law and medicine. Considering that matters of current litigation are almost always based in some degree on legal precedent, it is obvious that the law is fundamentally grounded in the exercise of abstraction. Judges, attorneys, and jury members must base their analysis of a given case on its relevant similarities to and differences from previously adjudicated cases. The second example, medicine, often requires the exercise of abstraction, as an analysis of making diagnoses shows. First, the physician must identify a number of diseases that share similar symptomatology. This number must then be reduced to one, or perhaps a few, by examining the similarities and differences between the pattern of symptoms presented by the patient and those that are typical of a given medical problem.

Although individuals are selected into occupations on the basis of their skills, it seems no less true that complex job tasks stimulate, demand, and exercise higher levels of abstraction and that this dynamic helps to develop and maintain this mode of thought. And of course the opposite argument can be made for routine and mundane jobs. In the analyses to follow we will test these hypotheses. We will also see whether there is a significant overall relationship between age and occupational complexity because, if so, this too could spuriously contribute to the age-abstraction association.

If occupational activities have important effects on the intellectual functioning of adults, it would follow that the timing of the onset of retirement has significant bearing on the complexity of older adults' daily environments and thus on the opportunities available to them for intellectual stimulation. If retirement is negatively associated with abstraction then this too can help explain part of the age-related decline in abstraction (as we can anticipate that age and retirement vary directly). Another labor force status with possible ramifications for abstraction is work in the home. Is the abstraction performance of housewives, as a group, significantly different from that of employed respondents, net of the other variables discussed thus far?[3]

4.5.2. Measures

Age was reported by respondents at the time of the interview. The data reflect that older people tend to round up or down to an even decade (70 or 80) or half-decade (75 or 85), which confirms that measurement is rarely if ever error-free.

The home environment in which a person was raised and socialization experiences from their childhood are indicated with a single variable called *highest*

[3]Without a measure of individual differences in the complexity of unpaid work in the home, an answer to a question at this level of generality must suffice.

parental education, or *parent's education* for short.[4] Admittedly this is a proxy for the complexity of the childhood environment, but without more detailed measures, parents' education is perhaps the best single indicator of social class differences in parental values and practices.

Respondent's education is the number of years of formal education a respondent had completed at the time of the interview. Of course it is somewhat unrealistic to assume that the effect of 1 year of education on abstraction is the same across time (i.e., between cohorts) or across people and schools at a single point in time. Nevertheless, without detailed measurement of the complexity of cumulative educational experience, the total number of years of formal educational attainment is our best single indicator.

Occupational complexity is based on information provided by respondents about the nature of their job and the industry in which they work. Those who were not employed at the time of the interview (approximately 45% of the sample) reported on the basis of the job that they had held the longest during their career of paid employment. This information was used to generate 1970 Bureau of the Census occupational status codes, which in turn were transformed into U.S. Employment Service data, people, and things complexity scores (Miller, Treiman, Cain, & Roos, 1980, Table F-1). For index building purposes, several combinations of complexity scores were formed. Using strength of association with abstraction as the criterion, it was decided that an additive scale combining complexity of work with people and data should be used in the analyses reported here.[5] Although this measure of occupational complexity is a considerable improvement over simpler classifications, such as the distinction between high- and low-status occupations, or the four-tier upper white collar, lower white collar, upper blue collar, lower blue collar occupational classification, it does not distinguish length of time on the job or length of time since the respondent was employed in the job.

Labor force status is measured as a set of dichotomous variables: retired, unemployed, and disabled respondents are coded 1 on "labor 1"; housewives are coded 1 on "labor 2"; and the currently employed are coded 0 on both (making them the omitted, comparison group). The results reported next are derived using multiple regression and path analysis techniques (e.g., Alwin & Hauser, 1975).

---

[4]An alternative variable based on the average educational attainment of both parents and another one based on the mother's years of education do not correlate as highly with abstraction as the variable used here. This supports the assumption that the parent with the highest education has the greatest impact on the stimulus complexity of the childhood environment. In most cases respondents were raised by two parents but in single-parent families the score on this variable is simply the educational attainment of the parent who raised the respondent.

[5]Work with data is classified from simple to complex as involving: comparing, copying, computing, compiling, analyzing, coordinating, and synthesizing. Similarly, work with people is ranked as follows: taking instructions and helping, serving, speaking and signaling, persuading, diverting, supervising, instructing, negotiating, and mentoring. (For more details see Miller et al., 1980, p. 22.)

4.5.3. Analyses and Results

Figure 4.1 (see p. 70) is the simplest and most efficient way to summarize the hypotheses discussed above. The number on each path between variables indicates the direction and amount of change in the dependent variable (notice there are five dependent variables in this model) per unit change in the independent variable, net of all other variables that affect it. Although all relationships are expressed in the same metric (standard deviations), these figures are not strictly comparable with respect to size.[6] The results obtained are evaluated as either supporting or contradicting the hypotheses on the basis of whether relationships are significantly different from zero and whether they are in the anticipated direction.

The direct relations between parent's education and abstraction (.120), respondent's education and abstraction (.230), occupational complexity and abstraction (.124), and retirement and abstraction (−.068, −.064) support their associated hypotheses. More generally, they provide unanimous support for the middle-range theory that environmental complexity stimulates intellectual functioning, as measured here with abstraction. Labor 2 has the only nonsignificant direct relationship with abstraction, which means that housewives' abstraction performance is not significantly different from that of currently employed respondents.

Finally, we can evaluate the relationship between age and abstraction net of the confounding influence of childhood environmental conditions, educational attainment, occupational complexity, and retirement. The direct path between age and abstraction is negative (−.123) and statistically significant at the $p < .01$ level. Although this does not mean that abstraction declines with age for everyone in the sample—indeed, it may increase for some individuals—it does reflect a general downward trend, although not as precipitous a fall as the bivariate relationship might lead one to believe.

Figure 4.1 presents information about several indirect routes through which age and sources of environmental complexity influence abstraction. Nondirect causation exists because the set of variables specified here are related to one another as well as to abstraction. Indeed, a positive manifold of status-related effects on abstraction begins with having highly educated parents, which leads to higher educational attainment, which leads to greater occupational complexity—and now we know that each of these factors has a direct effect on abstraction. Furthermore, the estimates of Figure 4.1 show that being highly educated and

[6]The existence of moderate to high correlations among a few of the variables inflates the estimates of their standard errors, thereby rendering comparisons invalid (Alwin, 1988b). An alternative procedure for evaluating the relative importance of the components of the model is the comparison of their total effects (age, .218; parent's education, .240; respondent's education, .322; occupational complexity, .142; retirement [labor 1], .064; housewife [labor 2], .068). On the basis of such comparisons one can conclude, for example, that respondent's education has 1½ times the total effect of age (.322/.218). The text, however, focuses on the specific paths through which these variables directly and indirectly influence abstraction. For present purposes, then, the criterion of relevance is less the magnitude of a relationship than its statistical significance.

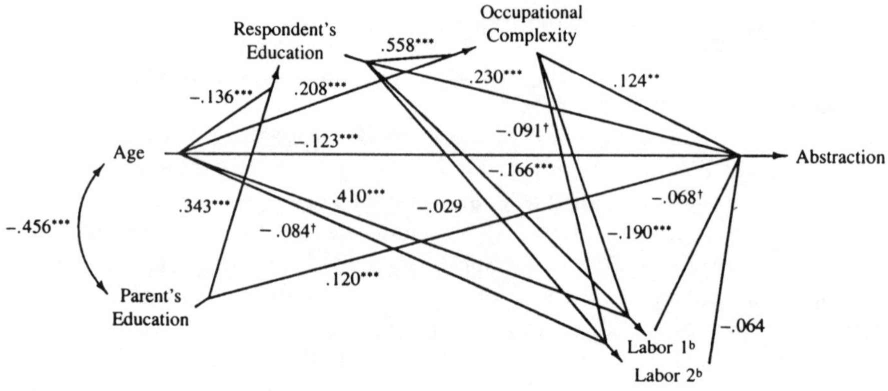

a*** = $p \leq .001$ ** $p \leq .01$ * $p \leq .05$ † $p \leq .10$.
bLabor 1: 1 = retired, unemployed, disabled 0 = else; Labor 2: 1 = "just not working" (housewives) 0 = else; Omitted: 1 = currently employed and students 0 = else.

FIGURE 4.1 Causal model of abstraction as influenced by age and social factors (numerical values are standardized partial regression coefficients[a]).

performing complex job tasks are negatively associated with retirement, which is itself related to lower abstraction performance. Thus, postponing retirement joins those conditions of environmental complexity that are positively related among themselves and that also positively influence abstraction. Because the variables that make up this positively inter-related system of determinants of abstraction are negatively related to age, age itself is often spuriously seen as the cause of lower intellectual performance among the elderly. But we have seen that in the sample as a whole, a considerable portion of the age-related deficit observed in Figure 2.1 is because older people were raised in less complex environments and have less formal educational experience, that these factors are associated with employment in less complex jobs, and that older people are more likely to be retired. All of these conditions are more prevalent among the elderly and all have negative associations with abstraction. It *is* interesting to learn, however, that a small part of the overall relationship between age and abstraction is positive. This is because, net of educational attainment and the other variables, age is positively related to job complexity.

4.6. Environmental Complexity of Elders: Retirement and Social Isolation

Although most evidence supporting the proposition that complex environments facilitate cognitive functioning comes from research on the early and middle stages of the life course, increasingly researchers are analyzing the cognitive functioning of elderly persons as a response to environmental conditions as well. Thus, as Schooler (1984, pp. 268–270) readily recognizes, the theory of the psychological effects of complex environments seems to be relevant across the life course. It will be recalled that Schaie (1983) and others (Arbuckle et al., 1986; Schaie & Willis, 1986) attribute the maintenance of cognitive skills into old age as due to participation in a stimulating, complex environment and leading an engaged life style; in short, to maintaining opportunities for intellectual stimulation.

If the family environment and schooling are the major sources of intellectual stimulation for youth, and if work is the primary source of cognitive demand in early and middle adulthood, then what comparable sources of stimuli are available to elders? Of course, continuing to work in paid employment sustains exposure to occupational sources of intellectual stimulation. Thus, postponing retirement is one means of maintaining cognitive demand in the later years of life. Nevertheless, surviving elders retire at some point and retirement is often seen as a major life event of old age.

> Retirement is considered one of the most important events for older workers. It clearly affects the way elders spend their time, the amount of their income, and who [sic] they interact with. It also has been assumed to affect their physical and mental health, self-esteem, happiness, and life satisfaction [Palmore, Fillenbaum, & George, 1984, p. 109; see also Atchley, 1976; Morgan, 1981; Palmore, 1971; Palmore, George, & Fillenbaum, 1982].

Labouvie-Vief (1985, p. 518) suggests that retirement "might well explain part of the apparently more normative declines in cognitive functioning in the late 60s to early 70s" because it causes a "dramatic constriction in economic and cultural participation and as such may often remove a viable supportive context" for maintaining cognitive abilities.

The analysis reported next focuses on the 177 respondents in the sample aged 55 to 88 years, who are hereafter designated "elders."[7] It asks whether retirement is associated with lower abstraction performance among elders, and if so, whether the abstraction scores of elders who supplant occupational sources of intellectual stimulation with alternative sources have abstraction scores more like employed elders than retired elders.

4.6.1. Hypotheses

The first hypothesis that can be tested with the available data is that retired elders tend to score lower on the abstraction index than employed elders. If this turns out to be the case, it may in part be due to selection; that is, individuals who suffer intellectual decrement choose to or are forced to resign earlier. But it is

---

[7]The primary reason for including the 55- to 64-year-old respondents in this analysis is to increase the size of the subsample.

also likely that part of such a retirement-related abstraction deficit could be explained along the lines of Labouvie-Vief's hypothesis that retirement removes a supportive context for maintaining intellectual functioning and thus leads to intellectual decrement.

A corollary to this hypothesis is that work-related sources of intellectual stimulation may be supplanted with alternative sources of cognitive demand and thus buffer the potentially negative impact of retirement on abstraction. We can test both hypotheses with the available data, but will have to be content with those alternative sources of stimulation that ensue from frequent social contact with close friends. Although it is known that participation in socially active environments is related to the cognitive performance of elderly adults (Arbuckle et al., 1986; Gribbon, Schaie, & Parham, 1980), it appears to be the *quality* or *intimacy* of interaction rather than the number of friends one has or the amount of interaction per se that matters (Larson, Zuzanek, & Mannell, 1985; Liang, Dvorkin, Kahana, & Mazian, 1980).

Thus, although it may be true that retired elders generally will have lower abstraction scores than employed elders, retirees who are engaged in frequent interaction with close friends should tend to have scores more nearly equal to those of employed elders than to their counterparts who are less active socially.

4.6.2. Measures

Fifty one respondents aged 55 to 88 years reported being currently employed at the time of the interview, whereas 126 elders were retired or disabled (the latter being the functional equivalent of retirement). A *labor force status* variable is thus dummy coded, 0 for currently employed and 1 for all others. An *interaction frequency* variable is developed from a series of questions respondents were asked about their three closest friends. In order to increase the likelihood that respondents reported reciprocal friendship relations (see Lauman, 1973) they were asked: "Now among all your good friends, think of three that you feel closest to and who also feel close to you. How often do you see [NAME OF FRIEND]?" The response options are: 5) almost daily, 4) 1–3 times per week, 3) 1–3 times per month, 2) 2–6 times per year, 1) less. In this way, frequency of contact with each reported friend was determined and scaled from 1 to 5, low to high contact. Adding scores across friends produces an index in which a high score indicates relatively frequent social contact.

4.6.3. Analyses and Results

In the sample as a whole, retired respondents score more than two full points lower on the abstraction index than employed respondents—a difference almost equal to one standard deviation. This, however, should not be taken as a true indication of the relationship between labor force status and abstraction because retirees are concentrated at the upper end of the age range (only eight retired respondents are younger than 60 years and more than three quarters of all retired respondents are older than 65 years). Because of this, various effects of age and age-related status factors on abstraction are confounded in the simple difference between retirees and employed respondents in the sample as a whole.

Narrowing the focus to respondents aged 55 to 88 years removes a large portion of the variation in age and correspondingly reveals a proportionately smaller difference (1.25 points, or about half a standard deviation) between employed and retired elders' abstraction scores. This is still not a genuine indication of the relationship between labor force status and abstraction, though, because even within this narrower age range retirees are, on average, about 10½ years older than employed elders. The best estimate of the relationship between labor force status and abstraction is obtained by statistically controlling variation in age as well as in the two education variables that are negatively related to age and positively related to abstraction. At the same time, in light of the corollary hypothesis regarding interaction frequency, this variable can be added to the equation.

Among these five predictors of abstraction (labor force status, age, respondent's education, parent's education, and interaction frequency), only two have statistically significant regression coefficients (in unstandardized form): respondent's education ($b = .134, p < .05$) and labor force status ($b = -.995, p < .05$). This means that even net of age and the other variables, retired elders score significantly lower on survey questions designed to measure abstraction than employed elders. The magnitude of this difference is equal to the improvement that is associated with an additional 7½ years of education (.995/134).[8] This clearly supports the hypothesis that retirement leads to decreased abstraction performance because it removes an important source of cognitive stimulation from everyday life.

The second hypothesis discussed above, which is actually a corollary of the first, is neither supported nor disproved by the finding that interaction frequency is not significantly related to the abstraction performance of elders as a whole because it specifically concerns the expected benefits of social sources of intellectual stimulation to retired elders only. In other words, whereas it is proposed that interaction frequency supplants the loss of occupation-related cognitive demand, no parallel expectation exists regarding employed elders. To test the corollary, a cross-product interaction term combining labor force status and interaction frequency is added to the equation specified above and new estimates are calculated. The total variance in abstraction explained by the equation including the interaction term is significantly greater ($p < .01$) than what is explained by the previous equation (15% compared to 10%).

Although we now know that the relationship between interaction frequency and abstraction differs for retired and employed elders, we do not know whether

[8]Note that net of labor force status, interaction frequency, and the two education variables, the association between age and abstraction is *not* statistically significant among elders.

it is stronger for one group than for the other but is in the same direction (a concordant interaction), or whether it is positive for one group of elders and negative for the other group (a discordant interaction). To answer this question the original equation is estimated separately for retired and employed elders. This analysis reveals a discordant interaction. The metric regression coefficient for interaction frequency among employed elders is $-.355$; among retired elders it is .102. Higher interaction frequency is associated with *lower* abstraction performance among employed elders, whereas higher interaction frequency is associated with *higher* abstraction performance among retired elders. (Each coefficient is larger than the respective coefficient for respondent's education, but only the first one is statistically significant at the .05 level.)

Insofar as abstraction is concerned, these results support the hypothesis that cognitive stimulation via frequent social contact with close friends supplants the loss of intellectual demand from retirement. Older adults who are retired *and* who have relatively little intimate social contact appear to suffer a cognitive deficit due to insufficient intellectual stimulation. This is entirely in keeping with the psychological effects of complex environments theory, and the metaphor of the mind-as-a-muscle, which follows the use-it-or-lose-it principle. It is perhaps somewhat surprising to learn that interaction frequency is negatively related to abstraction for employed elders—to find that less intimate social contact is better—but a similar finding is reported by Larson, Zuzanek, and Mannell (1985). They discover that being alone is a positive condition for retired adults who are married and that it is a negative condition for unmarried, retired adults. When alone, the married "reported greater arousal, concentration, and challenge, suggesting that they experienced aloneness as an occasion of deeper engagement in what they were doing" (p. 380). Similarly, the present study finds that infrequent social interaction is a condition of autonomy for elders who are actively engaged in intellectually demanding environments (as indicated by being employed). In contrast, among elders who are not engaged in occupational pursuits, infrequent social contact is more appropriately seen as a condition of isolation, as a life condition that compounds the retiree's disengagement from cognitively stimulating job tasks and work-related social contact. These results are consistent with the view that complex physical and social environments are needed to help adults maintain cognitive functioning into old age.

4.7. Environmental Complexity from Structural Overlap

Landecker's (1982) conception of structural overlap (based on the work of Simmel and Mannheim), Coser's (1975) conception of role complexity (based on the work of Merton), and Bronfenbrenner's (1979) conception of participation in multiple structural and cultural settings (based on the work of Lewin) share the view that environmental complexity contains the potential for positive developmental outcomes. Of course Landecker's (1982, p. 81) structural overlap hypothesis ("the experienced convergence, but not fusion, of shared and of discrepant affiliations will foster a tendency to distinguish between shared and discrepant properties—that is, to make abstractions") is the most explicit for our purposes. It guides the analyses undertaken next.

4.7.1. Hypotheses

It will be recalled that the sources of structural overlap are: status inconsistency, occupational mobility, heterogeneity in the family of origin, heterogeneity in the marital couple, diversity in the network of close friends, and living in a racially diverse neighborhood. Occupying different (inconsistent) vertical positions on two structural dimensions tends to result in greater exposure to status-based human diversity than is typically experienced by individuals with fully crystallized or consistent statuses. The same reasoning applies to occupational mobility, although in this case overlap is experienced sequentially rather than simultaneously. Religious, educational, and cultural differences in the family of origin provide additional opportunities to exercise and thus develop abstraction as a mode of thought. Furthermore, for the half of the sample that is married, since the marital couple is a point of convergence of two biographies, the greater the marital heterogeneity the greater the opportunity to observe differences among similarities and similarities among differences.

It also stands to reason that abstraction can be facilitated by having a diverse network of close fiends. A heterogeneous social network provides the opportunity to observe commonalities even in the presence of obvious differences between oneself and a friend and between friends—to know that at one level people are different while at another level they are alike. Finally, living in a neighborhood that is not entirely composed of residents with the same race is another source of structural overlap that, the structural overlap hypothesis suggests, should have a positive effect on abstraction.

Unlike the previous analyses, in which the two dimensions of abstraction were combined into a single index, the analyses reported below treat the two dimensions separately. This is because even though the experience of structural overlap is expected to foster the recognition of similarities among distinct objects, it may also provoke frustration that can be vented in the form of prejudice and stereotypes (see Landecker, 1980, p. 170; Lee, 1988, p. 141).[9] By analyzing the two dimensions of abstraction independently, we can separate potentially negative effects of structural overlap on nonstereotype thinking from the positive effects projected for nonconcrete thinking.

---

[9]If we recognize that at a more macrolevel the experience of structural overlap is equivalent to a low degree of class crystallization, then we must agree with Landecker (1980, p. 170) that "while it is hypothesized that a low degree of class crystallization, as a sociostructural factor, is conducive to the nonstereotypic use of categories, there is also reason to think that the same sociostructural factor has a sociopsychological counterpart with precisely the opposite effect."

A second difference between the analyses reported below and those reported earlier is that whereas gender interactions were not found in any of the preceding analyses, males and females do appear to respond differently to the experience of structural overlap. Evidence of gender-related role differentiation in small groups (Bales, 1958; Zelditch, 1955) and of gender differences in the giving and receiving of social support (Kessler & McLeod, 1984; Reis, Senchak, & Solomon, 1985; Stokes & Levin, 1986; Wheeler, Reis, & Nezlek, 1983) suggests that women are more attentive to interpersonal characteristics, especially in families and friendship networks. Thus, women may benefit from structural overlap more than men because they are more attentive to the objects of perception in which differences and similarities exist.

4.7.2. Measures

Four status dimensions—race/ethnicity, education, occupation, and personal income—are used to assess *status inconsistency* in the form of six pairwise status combinations. Each status dimension is expressed in four levels.[10] Only relatively large (i.e., two- and three-step) differences between an individual's positions on any pair of status dimensions are used as a positive indication of status inconsistency. Initially, a distinction was made between favorable and unfavorable status inconsistencies because it is known that there is a different psychological reaction to over-reward (viz., guilt) than to under-reward (viz., distress) (Homans, 1961). Thus, each of the six status inconsistency variables was coded as favorable, unfavorable, or consistent. However, detailed analyses based on each of these variables individually (reported in Lee, 1988, pp. 111–117) showed that the favorable/unfavorable distinction is not especially useful. Thus, for present purposes it is dropped, each variable is treated as a dichotomy, and the six variables are combined into a single *status inconsistency index.* A 0 indicates no experiences of status inconsistency and a 6 indicates the maximum number of status inconsistency experiences possible.

Generational occupational mobility is positively indicated by a two- or three-step difference between the respondent's current (or most recent) occupational status and the respondent's father's occupational status. *Personal occupational mobility* is a joint classification of respondents by their current occupation and the occupation they held for the longest time other than the present one. In the more detailed analysis reported in Lee (1988, pp. 118–122), each of these

[10]The race/ethnicity variable is a condensation of 80 categories into the following vertical scheme (low to high status): black; non-black, non-European; South and East European; and West and North European. The break points for education are: less than 12 years, high school graduate, some higher education but no college degree, and college graduate or higher. Occupations are classified using the 1970 Census Bureau scale of occupational status into lower blue collar, upper blue collar, lower white collar, and upper white collar categories. Personal income is classifed according to the average distribution of cases across the four levels of the education and occupation variables. The resultant categories are $400–7,000; $7,100–12,000; $12,500–25,000; and $26,000–99,000.

variables is treated individually and a distinction is made between upward mobility, downward mobility, and no mobility; however, for present purposes the upward and downward categories are combined (again because the distinction was not particularly useful). These two dichotomies are then used to form a single *occupational mobility index,* coded 0 for no mobility and up to 2 for individuals who had experienced both types.

Three variables, based on religion, education, and ethnicity, are used to indicate *heterogeneity in the respondent's family background.* Respondents were asked "What was your mother's religious preference while you were growing up?" and "Is your religious preference the same now?" Six categories were used to classify responses: Catholic and Orthodox, Protestant (all denominations), Jewish, nontraditional Christian, other, and no preference. A "no" response to the second question indicates religious heterogeneity in the respondent's background.[11] A second variable is based on the extent to which one's parents had different levels of educational attainment. An individual's standing on this variable is simply determined by the absolute value of the difference (in years) of the mother's and father's educational attainment. The third measure of structural overlap in the family of origin, ethnic heterogeneity, is based on the question, "Was either of your parents born outside of the U.S.?" Respondents who said "yes" are assumed to have some degree of multicultural experience. Each of these three variables is treated as a dichotomy and is used to form a single *index of structural overlap in the family background,* paralleling those discussed above and ranging from 0 to 3.

Marital religious heterogeneity is determined by comparing the respondent's religious preference with the spouse's mother's religious preference.[12] Another variable is derived from comparing the respondent's ethnic or nationality group identification (using about 40 different categories) with that of the spouse. A third and final indicator of structural overlap in the marital couple is whether or not there are substantial differences in the occupational statuses of the respondent's and the spouse's fathers. Using a four-tier (lower/upper, blue collar/white collar) occupational status scheme, heterogeneity in fathers' occupational statuses is indicated by two- and three-step differences. Each of these three indicators of marital structural overlap is coded 1 when a condition of heterogeneity is satisfied, otherwise a score of 0 is given. Unmarried respondents are assigned scores of 0 for these variables. A single *marital structural overlap index* is formed by adding these scores, which produces a variable ranging from 0 (no overlap) to 4 (maximum overlap).

---

[11]It is assumed that children are brought up in the mother's religion. Thus, if their religious preference had changed by the time of the interview then they are likely to have been exposed to the beliefs and customs of two religions, minimally. This experience would provide the opportunity to discover commonalities in different religious beliefs and practices.

[12]Unfortunately, the spouse's religious preference was not identified in the 1980 Detroit Area Study.

Five network structural overlap variables are formed from information provided by respondents concerning the age, occupational status, religion, years of educational attainment, and family income of each person named as one of their three closest friends. In 75% of the sample, the respondent and all friends shared the same 20-year age range. When a 20-year age difference was observed, either between the respondent and a friend or between two friends, a score of 1 was given for the age heterogeneity variable. The occupational heterogeneity variable gets a score of 1 when either two or three friends have different statuses compared to the respondent (the status categories used are blue collar, white collar, and housewife). Similarly, religious heterogeneity is scored 1 when either one, two, or all three friends have a different religion than the respondent. (About 50% of all respondents reported three friends who have the same religion as they have.) The education and income heterogeneity variables are coded alike. When all mentioned friends are "a little higher," "a little lower," or "the same" as the respondent (e.g., as compared to "much richer" or "much less education") then a score of 0 is given. About one half of the respondents are coded 0 for income and about three quarters are coded 0 for education. These five dichotomies, each of which is scored 1 when there is overlap and 0 when there is none, are added together to form a single *network structural overlap index,* ranging from 0 to 5.

The indicator of neighborhood racial diversity is based on the interviewer's judgment of the percentage of black families living on the respondent's block. The response categories are 0%, 1 to 9%, 10 to 49%, 50 to 74%, 75 to 94%, and 95% + . All but the first category are used to indicate exposure to racial diversity for whites, whereas all but the last category are used to indicate exposure to racial diversity for blacks.

4.7.3. Analyses and Results

If the measurement of structural overlap is detailed and somewhat complicated, the analyses based on the indices just described are relatively straightforward. Again using multiple regression, relationships between the structural overlap indices and each dimension of abstraction are estimated net of age, parent's education, respondent's education, occupational complexity, race, and gender. The results are presented in Table 4.4, which shows that all five structural overlap indices—status inconsistency, occupational mobility, and overlap in the family of origin, the marital couple, and the network of friends—are positively related to nonconcrete thinking, whereas the first three indices are negatively related and the last two are positively related to nonstereotype thinking. However, out of all of these relationships, only three are statistically significant (one at the .10 level and two at the .01 level).

Table 4.4 also presents selected results from the same analysis by gender. Notice that for males all five listed relationships are negative, whereas for females four out of the five are positive. Three of the five negative relationships for males are statistically significant and three of the four positive relationships

TABLE 4.4 Standardized partial regression coefficients of predictors of nonconcrete and nonstereotype thinking: Structural overlap analysis

	Nonconcrete	Nonstereotype
Control variables		
Age	−.182[a]	−.055
Respondent's education	.272[a]	.107[c]
Parent's education	.049	.123[b]
Occupational complexity	.072[d]	.142[b]
Race (white = 0)	−.102[b]	−.039
Gender (male = 0)	.053	−.028
N	579	579
R square	.20	.10
Structural overlap indices		
Status inconsistency	.048	−.103[b]
Occupational mobility	.017	−.037
Family background heterogeneity	.076[d]	−.011
Marital heterogeneity	.047	.026
Network heterogeneity	.100[b]	.021
N	563	563

	Nonconcrete		Nonstereotype	
Structural overlap indices	Males	Females	Males	Females
Status inconsistency	—	—	−.162[b]	−.048
Occupational mobility	−.092[d]	.116[c]	—	—
Family background heterogeneity	—	—	−.093[d]	.070
Marital heterogeneity	—	—	—	—
Network heterogeneity	−.008	.167[b]	−.036	.096[d]
N	258	305	258	305

[a] $p < .001$.
[b] $p < .01$.
[c] $p < .05$.
[d] $p < .10$.
[e] All relationships described in the second and third horizontal panels are net of age, respondent's education, parent's education, and occupational complexity.

for females are statistically significant. One of the strongest relationships revealed in these analyses is the tendency for males who experience status inconsistency to be more likely to think stereotypically ($b = -.162$, $p < .01$). Among the females in the sample the facilitation of nonconcrete thinking through the experience of network structural overlap is at least as strong ($b = .167$, $p < .01$). It is also noteworthy that the experience of occupational mobility tends to promote concrete thinking among males ($b = -.092$, $p < .10$) but nonconcrete thinking among females ($b = .116$, $p < .05$). The remaining comparisons listed in the bottom panel of Table 4.4 are in accordance with, although they provide less firm evidence for, the conclusion that the experience of structural overlap tends to foster one or the other (or in the case of network overlap, both) dimension of abstraction for women while having the opposite effect for men.

The relationship between exposure to racial diversity in the neighborhood and the two dimensions of abstraction is estimated net of age, parent's education, respondent's education and occupational complexity. Separate analyses by race show that exposure to racial diversity is positively related to nonstereotype thinking but is unrelated to nonconcrete thinking for blacks and whites alike.

4.8. Chapter Summary

Early in this chapter we observed that questionnaire items used in sample survey research should be based on widespread information, present manageable tasks, and use simple language and common concepts. In contrast to most of the abstraction and abstraction-related measures discussed in chapter 1, the five items used to measure nonconcrete and nonstereotype thinking in the 1980 Detroit Area Study satisfy these qualifications. The coding criteria for the nonconcrete items parallel the scoring guidelines of two of the most widely used measures of the recognition of similarities in the tests and measurement literature.

The psychometric properties of the abstraction index are fair to good. Certainly, there is enough response variation in the individual items to make explanation possible. Confirmatory factor analysis shows that the nonconcrete and nonstereotype dimensions of abstraction are validly distinguished by their respective indicators. Furthermore, the moderately high correlation between the two dimensions (factors) provides support for combining them into a single abstraction index. It is regrettable that the reliability of this index (alpha = .53) is not higher. Assuming the same interitem correlations, its reliability would be elevated to .71 if the number of items was doubled. But in view of the need for a measure that incorporates both dimensions of abstraction and is suitable for use in survey research, the one used here is satisfactory for the present purposes.

One such purpose was to estimate the relationship between age and abstraction net of birth cohort-related differences in exposure to sources of environmental complexity. It was found that some decline is typical for adults in general but that it is only about half as great as the deficit depicted in Figure 2.1. The other half is because members of earlier birth cohorts tend to have had less exposure to complex family, home, and educational environments than members of more recent birth cohorts. As part of the larger effort to provide social explanations for differences in psychological functioning—not just between cohorts but between individuals as well—it was observed that a positive manifold exists in the interrelations among family background, educational attainment, occupational complexity, the postponement of retirement, and abstraction. Thus, not only does a favorable location on one variable foster abstraction, but it also translates into a greater likelihood of occupying a favorable position in another context, which also fosters abstraction. For example, higher educational attainment has its own positive effect on abstraction and also leads to greater job complexity, which in turn facilitates abstraction. All in all, results from these analyses support the theory of the psychological effects of complex environments.

In a separate analysis of the elders in the sample, the normative age deficit in abstraction all but disappears when labor force status is controlled. Net of age and educational differences, retired elders tend to score lower on the abstraction index than employed elders. This suggests that retirement results in *disengagement* from the kind of environmental stimulation needed to support intellectual functioning into old age. It was learned, however, that job-related sources of cognitive demand can be supplanted with alternative forms of intellectual stimulation. Interaction with close friends appears to be one such alternate because the average abstraction score of retired elders who report relatively frequent interaction with close friends is not significantly different from that of the employed elders, whereas retired elders with relatively infrequent intimate social interaction score lower on abstraction than either of these subgroups, presumably because of insufficient intellectual stimulation. In sum, the evidence suggests that infrequent contact with close friends is a condition of social isolation among retired elders but is a condition of autonomy among employed elders, at least insofar as abstraction is concerned.

Data were also brought to bear on the structural overlap hypothesis, which proposes that the experience of shared but not fused social affiliations fosters the tendency to make abstractions. There was some support for this hypothesis but it is largely limited to the women in the sample. Among men the experience of some forms of structural overlap is associated with stereotype thinking, whereas among women structural overlap tends to facilitate nonconcrete thinking. A possible explanation of these different outcomes is that women, generally speaking, are more conscious of and attentive to various aspects of familial and friendship groups, and thus are more aware of differences and similarities in these groups. On the other hand, men typically are more concerned with status badges of various sorts, and thus certain types of structural overlap, particularly those of the negative variety incurred through status inconsistency and downward occupational mobility, tend to foster stereotyping among them.

Thus concludes this chapter on the analysis of data collected by the 1980 Detroit Area Study which, although far from ideal, has allowed us to bring some empirical evidence to bear on a number of the issues and hypotheses discussed in the preceding chapters. Various constraints on these conclusions are discussed in the following chapter.

5
The Study of the Social Bases of Intellectual Functioning Across the Life Course: Issues, Findings, and Directions for Further Research on Abstraction

5.1. Introduction

The study of the social bases of intellectual functioning across the life course faces three broad challenges: (a) *the conceptualization* and *measurement* of intellectual functioning, (b) the *identification* of genuinely causal relationships, and (c) the valid *generalization* of findings to a population of interest. This final chapter evaluates this study's response to each of these challenges, exposing the strengths and limitations of the theoretical orientations and methodological approaches that have guided this work. A summary of conclusions follows that and then the book concludes with a discussion of future directions in research on abstraction.

5.2. The Three Challenges

The three challenges of conceptual clarity and valid measurement, identification of causality, and generalization of findings typify social research more generally. In an insightful discussion of these challenges in terms of the scientific aims of realism, representation, and randomization, Kish (1987) shows that any actual study compromises at least one, and typically two of these aims in order to satisfy another. The classic experimental method randomly assigns subjects to treatment conditions, thus ensuring that measurable differences in outcome "y" are due to measurable differences in treatment "x." But causal certainty is often traded for somewhat sterile measures, the unrealistic environmental conditions of the laboratory, and low generalizability. On the other hand, whereas survey research usually suffices with the weaker method of statistical control to evaluate causality, results obtained using scientific sampling techniques can be generalized with a known degree of error to a large population. Field experiments are weaker on randomization than classic experiments and on representation than sample survey research, but are strong with respect to realism.

Although each of the three challenges concerns an integral and necessary part of the scientific enterprise, invariably compromises are made in any actual endeavor to test hypotheses against data. Being aware of these issues and compromises, and how they affect results, is basic to any research effort. In the subsections that follow each of the three challenges is discussed as it relates to the present study.

5.2.1. Conceptualization of Intelligence: The Case of Abstraction

For nearly a century psychologists have probed and grappled with the conceptualization and measurement of intellectual functioning. In broad terms, a given approach to this pursuit can be related to the ends the concept serves. Thus, as long as intelligence is thought of as wholly determined by genetic factors, the concept is used to justify the status quo, and the most valid measure of it is the existing, unequal distribution of resources and status positions. It follows, then, that those at the top of status hierarchies are the most intelligent. But the conceptualization and measurement of intelligence become much more complex when the dominant ideological functions of the concept are replaced by its use as a criterion for distributing scare opportunities and resources, and for evaluating educational programs and social mediation efforts.

The view that intellectual functioning is grounded in the nature of social experience, not just in early childhood but throughout life, is contrary to *fixed* conceptions of intelligence. A basic tenet of this orientation is that the very meaning of intelligent behavior undergoes transformation across time and varies across place. In this connection, a number of contemporary approaches to the conceptualization and measurement of intellectual functioning (mentioned in chapter 1) are welcome departures from many past efforts. Theories that specify multiple components of intelligence and microlevel analyses that focus on specific aspects of intellectual functioning do not claim to explain human intelligence in its entirety. These approaches are preferable to those based on reified and unitary conceptions of intelligence.

Although this study makes no pretense to investigate any facet of intellectual functioning other than abstraction, it does give this mode of thought a thorough scrutiny. It began by defining the term. This required distinguishing, first, between the literal and relational meanings of abstraction (both involve drawing away from objects of perception, but the latter also entails comparison); and second, between abstractness (or level of generality) and abstraction (a mode of thought). Next came a discussion of the conceptual relationships between abstraction and the theories of intelligence of Binet and Simon, Spearman, Thurstone, and Cattell. It was pointed out that whereas abstraction has an important role in such overarching theories, the way in which it is conceived of here accords more closely with contemporary componential and information processing approaches to intelligence. Following this, a fairly exhaustive overview of existing tests and measures of abstraction was conducted. These tests were assembled into a compendium according to whether they primarily serve clinical/psychiatric, educational, or multipurpose ends. Later it was concluded that although none of these tests is ideal for use in survey research, some are more useful than others. Indeed, the similarities questions and their coding guidelines provide models for the development of a better measure of abstraction for survey research purposes.

Abstraction is conceived of as classification on the basis of similarities and differences that, as theory and research in cognitive psychology indicates, is basic to the formation of new and inter-related concepts. Concept formation and development, in turn, is used to build increasingly complex knowledge structures. We saw that it would be mistaken to think that abstraction alone is sufficient to produce knowledge: abstraction is a way of thinking about content matter. It is important to distinguish *processes* of thinking *about* content matter from *qualities* of the content matter itself (such as its abstractness, complexity, substantive composition). It is no less important to realize that, however separate analytically, these two naturally co-occurring and interdependent components of "higher order thinking" cannot be pared off from one another in order to compare heir relative importance in learning generalization. The view adopted here is that learning content is every bit as important as learning to think critically and creatively about content. Undue emphasis on either is detrimental to the other, destructive of the natural and necessary balance between them, and ultimately harmful to learning and knowing.

After considering several examples of the use of abstraction in educational contexts and everyday life, it became apparent that the definition of abstraction as the detection of commonalities among objects of analysis needed refining. Certainly, abstraction is to be contrasted with undergeneralization, or seeing everything as distinct and particular with no common threads linking elements of experience and knowledge together in higher concepts. But this definition fails to recognize the other end of the generalization continuum. Overgeneralization entails the *disregard of relevant differences* which, additional conceptual analysis showed, is the essential definition of the concept of stereotyping. Thus, simply stating that abstraction involves similarity detection, while true and basic, is incomplete because it fails to distinguish abstraction from stereotyping—another mode of classification on the basis of similarities. Abstraction, then, entails detecting similarities among objects of analysis otherwise perceived as different, whereas stereotyping involves lumping all members of a group together on the basis of a shared attribute and rigidly disregarding, or failing to distinguishing among, individual members' relevant differences.

5.2.2. Identification of Causality

Of the three challenges under discussion, the most intractable to this study is the identification of genuinely causal relationships among age, social factors, and abstraction. This is because randomization of subjects across time of birth is logically impossible and across childhood socialization experiences, educational attainment, occupational complexity, and timing of retirement is equally, if not logically, impossible.

Given these constraints, the cross-sequential longitudinal study design allows the best assessment of age, period, and cohort effects on intellectual functioning across the life course. At present, however, most currently available longitudinal data on intellectual development have been collected from single cohorts, and this confounds age and period effects. Moreover, the nonrepresentativeness of these studies and the higher rate of attrition of "decliners" from them almost certainly bias results in the direction of intellectual stability over time.

With these limitations in mind, we concentrated on what could be learned about intellectual functioning across the life course from cross-sectional data. Even though all three sources of influence on abstraction—maturation, historical conditions, and social factors—are confounded in one-time data, this problem can be surmounted by specifying underlying causes, measuring these variables, and using statistical methods to derive independent and unbiased estimates of their effects. Of course this procedure is susceptible to several limitations in practice. Hypotheses regarding a matter as complex as intellectual functioning do not embrace all sources of influence, measurement is never perfect, and the statistical methods employed require assumptions that depart from real-life circumstances. However, as long as these limitations are recognized and conclusions are tempered accordingly, this approach can provide insights into the social bases of intellectual functioning across the life course.

The inability to estimate reciprocal effects of abstraction on its determinants puts definite limits on the conclusions that can be drawn from this study. Although the avowed purpose here has been to examine the social determination of intellectual functioning, it must also be acknowledged that intellectual functioning itself influences the very conditions examined as its causes. For example, a respondent's education fosters abstraction, but it is also likely that prior abstraction ability facilitates later educational attainment. In the analyses reported in chapter 4, it is assumed that the direct relationship between these two variables reflects only the former direction of causation, but, admittedly, this is unrealistic. Persons more facile with abstraction typically choose to obtain a greater amount of education, as well as education of a higher quality. This process of selection also reflects the inequality of opportunity structures; that is, the more proficient have more opportunities that enable them to become even more competent and thus to have even more opportunities and so on. Similar hypotheses apply to the direct relations between abstraction and parent's education,[1] occupational complexity, time of retirement, interaction frequency, and structural overlap experience (but not age).

Although the results in chapter 4 are reported as "direct effects" of various social experiences on abstraction, this reflects the assumptions of the specified models that are constrained by the available data and the statistical procedures used. But the fact that these results are consistent with the hypothesis that individuals with a particular level of abstraction ability select and/or are selected

[1]Of course a child's facility with abstraction would rarely affect parental educational attainment, but it does influence how parents and other agents of socialization interact with the child. Recall that the parent's education variable is a proxy for childhood socialization experiences.

to have certain social experiences does not invalidate the conclusion that much of the evidence reported here supports—namely, the theory of the psychological effects of complex environments. Because cognition and social experience are bound up in a complex web of reciprocal determination, diametrically opposed conceptions of socialization and selection processes pose an unrealistic dilemma. From a life course perspective, socialization and selection processes are part of the same phenomena of interest. Indeed, if we know anything, it is that human beings are social players who both act and are acted upon, which is to suggest that we should conceive of socialization, along with E.O. Wilson (1980, p. 81), as "the sum total of social experiences that alter the development of an individual."

It should also be recognized that selection arguments isolated from socialization ones tend to be overly deterministic. It is much too limiting to assume that associations between social factors and intellectual functioning are ultimately due to the greater opportunities provided to individuals on the basis of their standing on those factors in the first place. But the argument that prior intellectual functioning determines current intellectual functioning must ultimately explain what determines prior intellectual functioning.

This book contributes no new insights to the debate about the relative contributions of the environment and genetics to the determination of intelligence. The fact that the anatomy, chemistry, and physiology of the brain are fundamental to intellectual functioning would lead one to believe that, to the extent that these things are influenced by an individual's genetic makeup, the latter may somehow function as a predisposing factor. Yet, strict genetic determination of intellectual functioning is unlikely, for the reason quoted in chapter 1 (see footnote 5): because "cell-to-cell connections in the brain are far too numerous and variable to be specified in detail by a person's genetic blueprint." Combinations of connections are strengthened through response to environmental stimulation. Because enough evidence has accumulated to show beyond any doubt that social factors make important contributions to intellectual functioning throughout the life course, the identification of these factors is an appropriate topic of research.[2]

5.2.3. Representation and the Generalization of Results

The inability to generalize research findings beyond the sample (or the antidote of assuming the existence of laws of psychological and social behavior) is a limitation of psychological experimentation (for examples, see Sears, 1987). However, when random sampling techniques are used to select units of analysis on which data are collected it is possible to generalize research findings within a known and limited amount of error to a much broader population of inference.

---

[2]Recall from chapter 2 that intellectual differences between same-aged respondents from different birth cohorts are found in repeated cross-sectional studies. As Baltes et al., (1984, p. 40) observe, these differences in level of measured intellectual functioning are not likely to be due to "biological or genetic differences between generations" so close together in time; instead, they are attributed to "differing environmental conditions."

Of the three challenges described in this section, representation is the least often addressed in studies of the social bases of intellectual functioning across the life course. One need only consider the dearth of researchers trained in sample survey methodology who investigate intellectual functioning (not attitudes) using the tools of their trade.[3] Nevertheless, an indication that the subject is deemed significant by survey researchers is that the General Social Survey (an annual, omnibus survey of the U.S. population) has been using a 10-item vocabulary test of "general intelligence" for years (Davis & Smith, 1987). The argument for using such a measure is that it is highly correlated with a number of widely used batteries of general intelligence (Miner, 1957). However, to people who study the social embeddedness of intellectual functioning, vocabulary skill as a single indicator of something so complex and multifaceted is likely to seem far too restrictive.

There is an increasing awareness among cognitive psychologists and survey researchers that their respective disciplines are complimentary in important ways (see, e.g., the earlier volume in the *Recent Research in Psychology Series* edited by Hippler, Schwartz, & Sudman, 1987). At present, however, it seems to be survey researchers who benefit from lessons of cognitive psychology more than the reverse. An obvious reason for this is that it is easier to modify how one asks questions (a contribution of cognitive psychology to survey research) than to change one's approach to collecting and analyzing data (the contribution of survey research to cognitive psychology). When due attention is given both to principles of cognitive psychology and survey research techniques, it is generally concluded that questionnaire items designed to measure intellectual functioning in a heterogeneous population should be crafted using simple language and common concepts, should be clear and straightforward, and should not make the respondent feel that he or she is being tested. These guidelines also dovetail with the idea of measuring a single dimension of intellectual functioning at a time. Although there is a need for measures that put a number of intellectual competencies together (particularly for purposes of educational or occupational evaluation), for the sake of analytic purity it is important to be able to focus on distinct

[3]It is on first thought curious that sociologists, for the most part, refrain from studying the social bases of intellectual functioning. There are, however, several reasons why this may be so. First, the sociological orientation discounts genetic factors in human affairs. Second, because the examination of race, ethnic, gender, religious, and other group differences is basic to sociological inquiry, a topic such as intellectual functioning that can be discussed in genetic terms is avoided. Third, perhaps sociologists refrain from studying human intelligence because historically it has been aligned with psychologists' realm of academic and business pursuits. The fact that the measurement of intelligence is a multimillion dollar industry may also contribute to sociologists' seeming disdain for the concept. Finally, psychometrics is somewhat foreign to most sociologists and this too may help explain why members of this discipline, who would seem to have a unique perspective to contribute, do not actively participate in the study of the social bases of intellectual functioning across the life course.

components of intellectual functioning. Thus, in this study of intellectual functioning using sample survey data, emphasis was placed first on defining abstraction with precision and then on developing measures in accordance with the above guidelines.

This takes us back to the second part of the first challenge: the measurement of intellectual functioning. Confirmatory factor analysis results suggested that the effort to measure abstraction in a random sample of adults was congruent with the theory-based rationale used to develop the indicators. The middling level of reliability of the index reflects the presence of a substantial amount of measurement error. That the results of the analyses were consistent with the hypotheses formulated, even in the presence of considerable measurement error in the dependent variable (which attenuates relationships), leads one to believe that stronger support is forthcoming in research that uses a more reliable measure of abstraction.

5.3. Conclusions from the Social Psychological Study of Abstraction and Age

Abstraction is the recognition of similarities in otherwise distinct objects, events, persons, situations, and so forth. In operational terms, it is jointly defined in contrast to concrete thinking, in which everything is seen as different, despite the existence of essential commonalities, and in contrast to stereotype thinking, in which everything is viewed as the same, despite the existence of relevant differences. Defined and operationalized as such, the concept of abstraction is not subject to reification as are unitary conceptions of intelligence and higher order thinking.

Abstraction is a basic form of categorization used to develop concepts inductively by classifying objects on the basis of similarities and differences. Such adjectives as difficult, abstruse, general, and impractical do not describe abstraction as a mode of thought, but rather the subject matter that is thought about. It is the content of thought that varies from simple and concrete to complex and abstract. A process of thought as basic as abstraction resists any such classification. Because abstraction is fundamental to thinking and learning, its role is obvious even in the early stages of cognitive development and it continues to play an important part in thinking throughout life.

Low levels of biological maturation and cumulative life experience set limits on intellectual functioning early in life. Whereas biological factors cannot be ruled out as facilitating or impeding cognitive development, there is incontrovertible evidence that social factors function as a catalyst or a hindrance to intellectual growth across the life course. This study found that social experiences in childhood and through all stages of adulthood are significantly associated with intellectual functioning in biologically mature individuals. In particular, class-based childhood socialization experiences, educational attainment, and occupational complexity are directly related to abstraction. The onset of retirement, the frequency of interaction with close friends, and the experience of structural overlap are also related to abstraction, but in more complicated ways. Evidence from the available data does not prove that these social conditions directly foster abstraction, but careful analysis of the results suggests that such a conclusion is valid.

This study finds that abstraction performance tends to decline somewhat across adulthood in a large and socially heterogeneous population. However, on the strength of the evidence reported here and elsewhere (e.g., Schooler, 1987) that complex environments foster intellectual functioning throughout the life course, it is reasonable to believe that the observed aging deficit can be moderated if not entirely prevented through the salubrious influence of engagement in complex environments. Indeed, age is not significantly related to abstraction performance in the subgroup of elderly respondents net of control variables (being retired vs. continuing to work after age 55 years, parent's and respondent's education, and interaction frequency).

An interesting and potentially useful finding suggested by the analysis of elders is that frequent contact with close friends buffers the negative consequences of retirement on abstraction.[4] On the other hand, there is some evidence to suggest that the same structural network condition is inversely related to abstraction among employed elders. These results caution against assuming that the existence or quantity of social relationships positively indicates social integration and negatively indicates social isolation. As long as the existence or number of ties and/or frequency of interaction has positive main or buffering effects on dependent variables of interest (e.g., psychological well-being, intellectual functioning, or physical health), then the negative connotation of the label "isolation" is appropriate for the lack of such ties or interaction. However, when infrequent contact with close friends is shown to be positively related to a favorable outcome (as it was in this study), the label "social autonomy" seems more valid (cf. Larson, Zuzanek, & Mannell, 1985).[5]

Finally, there were mixed results from tests of the structural overlap hypothesis. The prediction that the experience of shared affiliations with members of otherwise different groups promotes abstraction (or at least nonconcrete thinking) was borne out in a limited way among only the women of the study. It was interesting to find that some of the strongest support for this hypothesis was the positive relation between heterogeneity in the network of close friends and

---

[4]One may well ask whether cognitive decline determines the timing of retirement rather than results from it. In a review of seven longitudinal studies on the predictors of retirement, Palmore, George, & Fillenbaum (1982, p. 733) conclude that structural factors (socioeconomic status and job characteristics) are more important in accounting for the amount of employment, whereas both structural factors and subjective factors (self-reported health and attitudes) account for early retirement (before the age of 65 years).

[5]Likewise, the positive connotation of the concept of social support is contradicted when indicators of it are shown to be associated with negative outcomes (as, for example, in research on "the costs of caring" [Kessler & McLeod, 1984]).

women's abstraction performance. This outcome is consistent with previous research, which shows that women are more attentive than men to various interpersonal dimensions of social groups. Among men, however, there was a tendency for status inconsistency and occupational mobility (two types of structural overlap with unfavorable status combinations) to provoke greater stereotype thinking. It is possible that structural overlap is a frustrating experience under these circumstances and that stereotyping is a way to vent these feelings.

In view of the following considerations, it is perhaps surprising that any evidence was found in support of the structural overlap hypothesis at all. First, the fact that the two dimensions of abstraction were analyzed separately could only exacerbate the measurement problems discussed earlier. Second, the vast majority of people in modern societies are exposed to levels of social diversity not experienced by the mass of people living in previous eras. It must be remembered that early forms of the structural overlap hypothesis were developed to explain the influence of broad historical change on patterns or styles of thinking. Third, it may be that structural overlap conditions can have a positive influence on abstraction only when exposure to environmental complexity is lower than what was experienced by most of the respondents in this study. Additional empirical research is needed to explore this hypothesis together with Coser's (1975) view that role complexity produces positive outcomes and Bronfenbrenner's (1979) ideas concerning the developmental benefits from having heterogeneous social experiences.

5.4. Abstraction, Human Development, and the Concept of Differentiation: New Directions in Theory

This book has considered the relevance of abstraction to overarching theories of intelligence, to information processing and cognitive psychological orientations to intellectual functioning, to higher order thinking and to education more generally, to three somewhat distinct conceptual approaches to stereotyping, to class differences in social values and intellectual flexibility, to stages of cognitive development as described by Piaget, to issues in the sociology of knowledge, to the joint and separate consequences of retirement and frequency of social interaction, and to characteristics of friendship networks. The concept of abstraction has served admirably as a unifying theme around which these diverse concerns are organized. However, what is needed to guide further research on abstraction is an overarching theory of human development in which abstraction is an integral component of a system of significant, inter-related concepts. This final section sketches out such a framework based on Witkin et al.'s (1962) seminal treatise on psychological differentiation and human development. The purpose is simply to suggest in broad outline some possible directions for further research on abstraction in a more general developmental context.

The concept of differentiation, which concerns the complexity of a biological, psychological, or social system's structure, is the cornerstone of the highly integrative approach to human growth and development of Witkin and his colleagues. They maintain that *degree* of differentiation is reflected in how a system *functions* and that two functions of any system are *specialization* and *integration*. A highly differentiated psychological system, for example, is specialized. Specialization entails *separation* between psychological processes and areas (such as feeling and thinking) and *specificity* within an area (as when "parts of a perceptual field are experienced as discrete, rather than fused with their background"). Integration of a system "refers to the form of the functional relationships among system components and so speaks first of all on the patterning of the total system" (p. 10). *Effective* integration is the harmonious working together of parts into a whole and is reflected by adequacy of adjustment. *Complex* integration refers to the existence of complex relations between system components and between the system and the environment. Thus, complex systems are highly differentiated, which is to say that their component parts are specialized as well as integrated. Witkin et al. (pp. 6, 14) describe the implications of system complexity for human development as follows: "We may refer to the increasing discreetness of objects and to the use of more complex principles of field integration as an increase in the *articulateness of experience* . . . [G]reater or more limited articulation is a common quality that runs through much of a person's experience."

This theoretical framework, presented here in its barest form, is used to explain a remarkably consistent pattern of experimental results on perceptual, motivational, defensive, intellectual, and social operations. The earliest of these experiments employed rod and frame tests to measure the extent to which an individual depends on an embedding context to orient himself or herself in space. Additional research on field dependence, using, for example, the Embedded Figures Test and the Body Adjustment Test, indicates that this perceptual orientation is more generally characterized by difficulty in separating an object from its context and in structuring ambiguous stimuli. Field independence, on the other hand, is identified as the "ability to separate an item from its context," the "capacity to analyze experience," and as the organization or structuring of an internal or external field (p. 13). On the relation between perceptual and intellectual orientations, Witkin et al. write that what the analytic field approach has in common with intellectual activities "that call for a high degree of creative activity, but do not involve perception directly, [is that] both require that 'parts' be separated from the context in which they are embedded and brought into new relationships" (p. 59). Clearly, separating parts from embedding contexts requires abstraction, as defined literally, and to the extent that the separated parts are brought into new relationships on the basis of similarities and differences, this requires abstraction as defined in relational terms as well.

Developmentally, the greatest contrast in levels of differentiation is observed by comparing children to adults. Personal growth requires separating the self from the environment, gaining a sense of separate identity through discerning similarities and differences between self and others, developing greater determination from within, and becoming less reliant on external sources for nurturance, maintenance, and authority. These dynamics are summarized in Witkin et al.'s "differentiation hypothesis" which, at the conceptual level, relates progressive differentiation to greater articulation of experience. At the empirical level, articulateness is expressed in the analysis and structuring of experience, as indicated positively by measures of the analytic field approach (intellectual flexibility and valuation of self-directedness) and negatively by idea conformity and authoritarian conservatism (cf. Inkeles, 1983; Kohn, 1977; Kohn & Schooler, 1983). In general terms, it is believed that the achievement of a segregated, structured self provides internal frames of reference for viewing, interpreting, and dealing with the world from the position of an autonomous agency, which in turn is likely to aid in the development of an articulated way of experiencing the world.

Witkin and his colleagues combine theory and data in an overarching developmental orientation to the inter-relations among self, mind, and society. They recognize parallel structures and functions in biological, psychological, and social systems. Complex systems are differentiated, their components are specialized yet integrated. Systems and their parts are inter-related such that complexity in one system promotes, follows from, and is in equilibrium with complexity in another system. This book argues that abstraction follows from environmental complexity and promotes cognitive complexity. Additional theory and research may point to other forms of system complexity that are bound together in this positive manifold.

Bibliography

The Ann Arbor News. Abstract studies help students think clearly, researcher finds. (1987, November 5, p. 10).

Adorno, T. W., Frenkel-Brunswick, E., Levinson D. J., & Sanford, R. N. (1950). *The authoritarian personality.* New York: Harper.

Ahammer, I. (1973). Social learning theory as a framework for the study of adult personality development. In P. Baltes and K. W. Schaie (Eds.), *Life span developmental psychology. Personality and socialization* (pp. 253–284). New York: Academic Press.

Alfano, P. (1987, October 26). Latecomer becomes a fast finisher. *The New York Times.* p. 38.

Allport, G. W. (1954). *The nature of prejudice.* Reading, MA: Addison-Wesley.

Alwin, D. F., & Hauser, R. (1975). Decomposition of effects. *American Sociological Review 40,* 37–47.

Alwin, D. F. (1988). Measurement and the interpretation of effects in structural equation models. In J. S. Long (Ed.), *Common problems in quantitative social research.* Beverly Hills: Sage.

Alwin, D. F., Cohen, R., & Newcomb, T. (in press). *Aging, personality and social change: Attitude persistence and change over the life-span.* Madison: University of Wisconsin Press.

Anastasi, A. (1982). *Psychological testing* (5th ed.). New York: Macmillan.

Arbuckle, T. Y., Gold, D., & Andres, D. (1986). Cognitive functioning of older people in relation to social and personality variables. *Psychology and Aging 1,* 55–62.

Arenberg, D. (1968). Concept problem solving in young and old adults. *Journal of Gerontology* 23, 279–282.

Arendt, H. (1970). *On violence.* San Diego: Harcourt Brace Javanovich.

Arnhoff, F. N. (1956). Ethnocentrism and stimulus generalization. *Journal of Abnormal and Social Psychology 53,* 138–139.

Ashmore, R. D. & Del Boca, F. K. (1981). Conceptual approaches to stereotypes and stereotyping. In D. L. Hamilton (Ed.), *Cognitive processes in stereotyping and intergroup behavior* (pp. 1–36). Hillsdale, NJ: Lawrence Erlbaum.

Atchley, R. (1976). *The sociology of retirement.* Cambridge, MA: Schenkman Publishing Co.

Bachman, J. (1987). Declining marijuana use: The attitude-behavior connection. Paper presented at the Social Psychology Brown Bag Series, Department of Sociology, The University of Michigan, Ann Arbor, MI.

Bales, R. F. (1958). Task roles and social roles in problem-solving groups. In E. Maccoby, T. Newcomb, & E. Hartley (Eds.), *Readings in social psychology* (3rd ed.). New York: Holt, Rinehart, & Winston, Inc.

Baltes, P. B., Dittmann-Kohli, F., & Dixon, R. (1984). New perspectives on the development of intelligence in adulthood: Toward a dual process conception and a model of selective optimization with compensation. *Life-span development and behavior* 6, 33–71.

Bernstein, B. (1971–1973). *Class, codes, and control* (Vols. 1–3). London: Routledge & Kegan Paul.

Bettelheim, B. & Janowitz, M. (1964). *Social change and prejudice.* New York: The Free Press.

Bolton, N. (1977). *Concept formation.* Oxford, England: Pergamon Press.

Bortner, M. (1965). Review of the progressive matrices. In O. W. Buros (Ed.), *The sixth mental measurements yearbook.* Highland Park, NJ: Gryphon Press.

Botwanick, J. (1977). Intellectual abilities. In J. E. Birren & K. W. Schaie (Eds.), *Handbook of the psychology of aging* (2d ed). (1985). New York: Van Nostrand Reinhold.

Botwanick, J. (1978). *Aging and behavior.* New York: Springer-Verlag.

Bourne, L. E., Jr. (1966). *Human conceptual behavior.* Boston: Allyn & Bacon.

Bowlby, J. (1980). *Attachment and loss. Vol. III: Loss: Sadness and depression.* London: Hogarth Press.

Brief, J. C. (1983). *Beyond Piaget. A philosophical psychology.* New York: Teachers College Press.

Brody, E. B. & Brody, N. (1976). *Intelligence. Nature, determinants, and consequences.* New York: Academic Press.

Bromley, D. B. (1974). *The psychology of human aging.* Middlesex, England: Penguin.

Bronfenbrenner, U. (1979). *The ecology of human development.* Cambridge: Harvard University Press.

Buros, O. K. (Ed.). (1961–1983; inclusive). *Tests in print (I–III).* Highland Park, NJ: Gryphon Press.

Buros, O. K. (Ed.). (1938–1985; inclusive). *The mental measurements yearbooks.* Highland Park, NJ: Mental Measurements Yearbook.

Byron, G. G. B. (1885). *Childe Harold.* H. F. Tozer (Ed.). Oxford: Clarendon Press.

Carlsson, G. & Karlsson, K. (1970): Age, cohorts and the generation of generations. *American Sociological Review, 35*(4), 710–718.

Cattell, R. B. (1963). Theory of fluid and crystallized intelligence: A critical experiment." *Journal of Educational Psychology 54,* 1–22.

Cicirelli, V. G. (1976). Categorization behavior in aging subjects. *Journal of Gerontology 36,* 676–680.

Clement, J. (1982). Students' preconceptions in introductory mechanics. *American Journal of Physics 50,* 66–71.

Condemned killer says he can't get a fair deal. (1986, March 30). *The New York Times.*

Converse, J. & Presser, S. (1986). *Survey questions. Handcrafting the standardized questionnaire.* Sage University Paper series on Quantitative Applications in the Social Sciences, series no. 07–063. Beverly Hills: Sage Publications.

Converse, P. E. (1964). The nature of belief systems in mass publics. In D. Apter (Ed.), *Ideology and discontent.* Reprinted in abridged form in W. Gamson & A. Modigliani, *Conceptions of social life: A text-reader for social psychology.* 1979. Washington, DC: University Press of America.

Cormier, S. M. & Hagman, J. D. (Eds.). (1987). *Transfer of learning.* New York: Academic.

Coser, R. L. (1975). The complexity of roles as a seedbed of individual autonomy. In L. A. Coser (Ed.), *The idea of social structure* (pp. 237–251). New York: Harcourt Brace Jovanovich.

Cunningham, W. R. & Birren, J. E. (1980). Age changes in the factor structure of intellectual abilities in adulthood and old age. *Educational and Psychological Measurement* 40, 271–290.

Cunningham, W. R. & Owens, W. R. (1983). The Iowa state study of the adult development of intellectual abilities. In K. W. Schaie (Ed.), *Longitudinal studies of adult psychological development.* New York: The Guilford Press.

Davis, J. A. & Smith T. W. (1987). *General social surveys, 1972–1987: Cumulative codebook.* Chicago: NORC, University of Chicago.

Denney, N. W. (1974). Classification abilities in the elderly." *Journal of Gerontology, 29,* 309–314.

Douglas, M. (1970). *Natural symbols.* New York: Vintage.

Durkheim, E., & Mauss, M. (1963) *Primitive classification.* (R. Needham, Trans.). Chicago: University of Chicago Press. (Original work published 1903).

Egeland, B. (1985). Review of the Wisconsin card sorting test." In J. V. Mitchell (Ed.), *The ninth mental measurements yearbook.* Lincoln, NB: Buros Institute of Mental Measurement of the University of Nebraska.

Eells, K., Davis, A., Havighurst, R., Herrick, J., & Tyler, R. (1951). *Intelligence and cultural differences.* Chicago: University of Chicago Press.

Encyclopaedia Britannica. 1911 ed., s.v. Abstraction.

Encyclopaedia Britannica. 1983 ed., s.v. Abstraction.

Fienberg, S. E., & Mason, W. M. (1985). Specification and implementation of age, period and cohort models. In W. M. Mason & S. E. Fienberg (Eds.), *Cohort analysis in social research.* New York: Springer-Verlag.

Findlay, D. & McGuire, C. (1957). Social status and abstract behavior. *Journal of Abnormal and Social Psychology 54,* 135–137.

Fishman, J. A. (1956). An examination of the process and function of social stereotyping. *The Journal of Social Psychology 43,* 27–64.

Gardner, H. (1983). *Frames of mind. The theory of multiple intelligences.* New York: Basic Books.

Glaser, R. (1984). Education and thinking. *American Psychologist 39(2),* 93–104.

Glenn, N. D. (1981a). The utility and logic of cohort analysis. *The Journal of Applied Behavioral Science 17,* 247–257.

Glenn, N. D. (1981b). Age, birth cohorts, and drinking: An illustration of the hazards of inferring effects from cohort data. *Journal of Gerontology 36,* 362–369.

Goldstein, K. (1963[1940]). *Human nature in the light of psychopathology.* New York: Schocken Books.

Goldstein, K. & Scheerer, M. (1941). Abstract and concrete behavior: An experimental study with special tests. *Psychological Monographs 53(2),* 1–151.

Gorham, D. R. (1956). A proverbs test for clinical and experimental use. *Psychological Reports 2,* 1–12.

Gould, S. J. (1981). *The mismeasure of man.* New York: W.W. Norton & Co.

Graham, J. R. & Lilly, R. (1984). *Psychological testing.* Englewood Cliffs: Prentice-Hall.

Gregory, R. L. (1987). Piaget. In R. Gregory (Ed.), *The Oxford companion to the mind.* Oxford: Oxford University Press.

Gribbon, K., Schaie, K. W., & Parham, I. (1980). Complexity of life style and maintenance of intellectual abilities. *Journal of Social Issues 36,* 47–61.

Guilford, J. P. (1954). *Psychometric methods.* New York: McGraw-Hill.

Hartley, A. A. (1981). Adult age differences in deductive reasoning processes. *Journal of Gerontology 36,* 700–706.

Hellerstein, D. (1988, May 23). Plotting a theory of the brain. *The New York Times Magazine.* Pp. 16–19, 27, 28, 55, 61, 64.

Hippler, H. J., Schwartz, N., & Sudman, S. (Eds.). (1987). *Social information processing and survey methodology.* New York: Springer-Verlag.

Holland, J. H., Holyoak, K. J., Nisbett, R. E., & Thagard, P. R. (1986). *Induction. Processes of inference, learning, and discovery.* Cambridge, MA: The MIT Press.

Holyoak, K. J. (1984). Analogical thinking and human intelligence. In R. J. Sternberg (Ed.), *Advances in the psychology of human intelligence* (Vol. 2). Hillsdale, NJ: Lawrence Erlbaum.

Homans, G. C. (1961). *Social behavior. Its elementary forms.* New York: Harcourt Brace Jovanovich.

Horn, J. L. & Donaldson, G. (1976). On the myth of intellectual decline in adulthood. *American Psychologist 31,* 701–709.

House, J. S. (1977). The three faces of social psychology. *Sociometry 40*(2), 161–177.

House, J. S. (1981). Social structure and personality. In M. Rosenberg & R. H. Turner (Eds.), *Social psychology. Sociological perspectives* (pp. 525–561). New York: Basic Books.

Huber, J. & Form, W. (1973). *Income and ideology.* New York: Free Press.

Hunt, W. A. (1949). Review of the Shipley-institute of living scale for measuring intellectual impairment. In O. K. Buros (Ed.), *The third mental measurements yearbook.* New Brunswick, NJ: Rutgers University Press.

Inhelder, B. & Piaget, J. (1958). *The growth of logical thinking from childhood to adolescence.* New York: Basic Books.

Inkeles, A. (1983). *Exploring individual modernity.* New York: Columbia University Press.

Inkeles, A. & Smith, D. (1974). *Becoming modern: Individual change in six developing countries.* Cambridge: Harvard University Press.

Ives, M. (1949). Review of the Shipley-institute of living scale for measuring intellectual impairment. In O. K. Buros (Ed.), *The third mental measurements yearbook.* New Brunswick, NJ: Rutgers University Press.

Jarvik, L. F. & Bank L. (1983). Aging twins: Longitudinal psychometric data. In K. W. Schaie (Ed.), *Longitudinal studies of adult psychological development (pp. 40–63).* New York: The Guilford Press.

Jones, H. E. (1959). Intelligence and problem solving. In J. E. Birren (Ed.), *Handbook of aging and the individual.* Chicago: University of Chicago Press.

Joreskog, K. G. & Sorbom, D. (1988). *LISREL 7: A guide to the program and applications*. Chicago: SPSS.

Katz, D. & Braly, K. (1933). Racial stereotypes of one hundred college students. *Journal of Abnormal and Social Psychology 28*, 280–290.

Kelly, D. & Krueger, J. (1984). The psychology of abstraction. *Journal for the theory of social behavior 14*, 43–67.

Kessler, R. & McLeod J. (1984). Sex differences in vulnerability to undesirable life events. *American Sociological Review 49*, 620–631.

Kish, L. (1987). *Statistical design for research*. New York: John Wiley & Sons.

Kogan, N. (1974). Categorizing and conceptualizing styles in younger and older adults. *Human Development 17*, 218–230.

Kohn, M. L. (1977). *Class and conformity. A study in values* (2nd ed.). Chicago: The University of Chicago Press.

Kohn, M. L. & Schooler, C. (1983). *Work and personality: An inquiry into the impact of social stratification*. Norwood, NJ: Ablex.

Kundera, M. (1988, March 6). Key Words, Problem Words, Words I Love. *The New York Times Book Review*, pp. 1, 24–26.

Labouvie-Vief, G. (1985). Intelligence and cognition. In J. E. Birren & K. W. Schaie (Eds.), *Handbook of the Psychology of Aging* (pp. 500–530). New York: Van Nostrand Reinhold Co.

Landecker, W. S. (1981). *Class crystallization*. New Brunswick, NJ: Rutgers University Press.

Landecker, W. S. (1982). The use of survey research in the sociology of knowledge. *Knowledge: Creation, Diffusion, Utilization 4*(1), 73–94.

Larson, R., Zuzanek, J., & Mannell, R. (1985). Being alone versus being with people: Disengagement in the daily experience of older adults. *Journal of Gerontology 3*, 375–381.

Laumann, E. O. (1973). *Bonds of pluralism: The form and substance of urban social networks*. New York: Wiley Interscience.

Lee, J. S. (1988). *On abstraction: A sociological analysis*. Unpublished doctoral dissertation, University of Michigan.

Lee, J. S. & Landecker, W. S. (1989). Structural overlap and abstraction: A Simmel—Mannheim hypothesis. Unpublished manuscript.

Levinson, D. J. & Sanford, R. N. (1944). A scale for the measurement of anti-semitism. *Journal of Psychology 17*, 339–370.

Lewin, K. (1935). *A dynamic theory of personality*. New York: McGraw-Hill.

Liang, J., Dvorkin, L., Kahana, E., & Mazian, F. (1980). Social integration and morale: A re-examination. *Journal of Gerontology 35*, 746–757.

Lippmann, W. (1922). *Public opinion*. New York: Harcourt, Brace & Co.

Luria, A. R. (1976). *Cognitive development. Its cultural and social foundations*. (M. Lopez-Morillas and L. Solotaroff, Trans.). Cambridge, MA: Harvard University Press. (Original work published 1974.)

Manis, M., Nelson, T., & Shedler, J. (1988). Stereotypes and social judgment: Extremity, assimilation, and contrast. *Journal of Personality and Social Psychology 55*(1), 28–36.

Mannheim, K. (1936). *Ideology and utopia: An introduction to the sociology of knowledge* (L. Wirth & E. Shils, Trans.). New York: Harcourt, Brace, & World, Inc.

Mannheim, K. (1952). The sociological problem of generations. In P. Kecskemeti (Ed.), *Essays on the sociology of knowledge* (pp. 276–320). New York: Oxford University Press.

Martin, W. T. (1967). Analysis of the abstracting function in reasoning using an experimental test. *Psychological Reports 21,* 593–598.

Marzanio, R. J. & Hutchins, C. L. (1985). *Thinking skills.* Aurora, CO: Mid-continent Regional Educational Laboratory.

Matarazzo, J. D. (1972). *Wechsler's measurement and appraisal of adult intelligence* (5th ed.). New York: Oxford University Press.

Mayer, R. E. (1983). *Thinking, problem solving, cognition.* New York: W. H. Freeman & Co.

McCauley, C. & Stitt, C. L. (1978). An individual and quantitative measure of stereotypes. *Journal of Personality and Social Psychology 36,* 929–940.

McCauley, C., Stitt, C. L., & Segal M. (1980). Stereotyping: From prejudice to prediction. Psychological Bulletin 87, 195–208.

Merton, R. K. (1949). *Social theory and social structure: Toward the codification of theory and research.* Glencoe, IL: The Free Press.

Merton, R. K. (1967). *On theoretical sociology.* New York: The Free Press.

Miller, A. R., Treiman, D. J., Cain, P. S., & Roos, P. A. (Eds.). (1980). *Work, jobs, and occupations: A critical review of the dictionary of occupational titles.* Washington, DC: National Academy Press.

Miller, G. A. (1986). Explanatory skills. Paper commissioned by The Study Group on the National Assessment of Student Achievement.

Miller, J., Slomczynski, K. M., & Kohn, M. L. (1985). Continuity of learning-generalization: The effect of job on men's intellective process in the United States and Poland. *American Journal of Sociology 91,* 593–615.

Miller, K. A., Kohn, M., & Schooler, C. (1985). Educational self-direction and the cognitive functioning of students. *Social Forces 63,* 923–944.

Miller, K. A., Kohn, M. & Schooler, C. (1986). Educational self-direction and personality. *American Sociological Review 51,* 372–390.

Mills, C. W. (1959). *The sociological imagination.* New York: Oxford University Press.

Miner, J. B. (1957). *Intelligence in the United States.* New York: Springer; reprint Westport, Conn.: Greenwood, 1973.

Morgan, J. (1981). Antecedents and consequences of retirement. In M. Hill, O. Hill, & J. Morgan (Eds.), *5,000 American families* (vol. 9) Ann Arbor, MI: Institute for Social Research.

National Academy of Education (1987). *The Nation's report card. Improving the assessment of student achievement.* Cambridge, MA: National Academy of Education.

National Assessment of Educational Progress (1983). *The third national mathematics assessment: Results, trends and issues* (13–MA–01). Denver, CO: Educational Commission of the States.

National Assessment of Educational Progress (1986a). *Math objectives 1985–86 assessment.* Princeton, NJ: Educational Testing Service.

National Assessment of Educational Progress (1986b). *Science objectives 1985–86 Assessment.* Princeton, NJ: Educational Testing Service.

National Science Board Commission on Precollege Education in Mathematics, Science and Technology (1983). *Educating Americans for the 21st century.* Washington, DC: National Science Board, National Science Foundation.

Neisser, U. (1967). Cognitive psychology. New York: Appleton-Century-Crofts.

Newell, A. & Simon, H. A. (1972). *Human problem solving.* Englewood Cliffs, NJ: Prentice Hall.

Nisbett, R. E. & Ross, L. (1980). *Human inference*. Englewood Cliffs, NJ: Prentice-Hall.

Owens, W. A. (1966). Age and mental abilities: A second adult follow-up. *Journal of Educational Psychology 57,* 311–325.

Palmore, E. B. (1971). Why do people retire? *Aging and Human Development 2,* 269–283.

Palmore, E. B., Fillenbaum, G., & George, L. (1984). Consequences of retirement. *Journal of Gerontology 1,* 109–116.

Palmore, E. B., George, L., & Fillenbaum, G. (1982). Predictors of retirement." *Journal of Gerontology 6,* 733–742.

Parks, C. W., Mitchell, D. B., & Perlmutter, M. (1986). Cognitive and social functioning across adulthood: Age or student status differences? *Psychology and Aging 3,* 248–254.

Payne, R. W. (1965). Review of the Goldstein-Scheerer tests of abstract and concrete thinking. In O. W. Buros (Ed.), *The sixth mental measurements yearbook.* Highland Park, NJ: Gryphon Press.

Perkins, D. N. & Salomon, G. (1989). Are cognitive skills context-bound? *Educational Researcher 18*(1), 16–25.

Piaget, J. (1981[1947]). *The psychology of intelligence.* Totowa, NJ: Littlefield, Adams & Co.

Piaget, J. (1965). *The moral judgement of the child.* (M. Gabain, Trans.). New York: The Free Press. (Original work published 1932.)

Pikas, A. (1966). *Abstraction and concept formation. An interpretative investigation into a group of psychological frames of reference.* Cambridge, MA: Harvard University Press.

Reagan's letter to Craxi. (1985, October 21). *The New York Times.*

Reese, H. W. & Rodeheaver, D. (1985). Problem solving and complex decision making. In J. E. Birren and K. W. Schaie (Eds.), *Handbook of the psychology of aging* (2nd ed.). New York: Van Nostrand Reinhold Co.

Reis, H. T., Senchak, M., & Solomon, B. (1985). Sex differences in the intimacy of social interaction: Further examination of potential explanations." *Journal of Personality and Social Psychology 5,* 1204–1217.

Resnick, L. B. (1987). *Education and learning to think.* Washington, DC: National Academy Press.

Reston, J. (1986, March 23). What Reagan lost. *The New York Times,* p. 23.

Riley, M. W. (1973). Aging and cohort succession: Interpretations and misinterpretations. *Public Opinion Quarterly 37,* 35–49.

Riley, M. W. (1987). Foreword: Why this book? In K. W. Schaie & C. Schooler (Eds.), *Social structure and aging: Psychological processes* (pp. xii–xv). Hillsdale, NJ: Lawrence Erlbaum.

Rokeach, M. (1948). Generalized mental rigidity as a factor in ethnocentrism. *Journal of Abnormal Social Psychology 43,* 259–278.

Rosch, E. (1978). Principles of categorization. In E. Rosch and B. B. Lloyd (Eds.), *Cognition and categorization,* pp. 27–48). Hillsdale, NJ: Lawrence Erlbaum.

Rosch, E. & Lloyd, B. B. (Eds.) (1978). *Cognition and categorization.* Hillsdale, NJ: Lawrence Erlbaum.

Rosch, E. & Mervis, C. B. (1975). Family resemblances: Studies in the internal structure of categories. *Cognitive Psychology 7,* 573–605.

Rosch, E., Mervis, C. B., Gray, W. D., Johnson, D. M., & Boyes-Braem, P. (1976). Basic objects in natural categories. *Cognitive Psychology* 8, 382–439.

Ryder, N. (1965). The Cohort as a Concept in the Study of Social Change. *American Sociological Review 30,* 843–861.

Salthouse, T. A. (1982). *Adult cognition. An experimental psychology of human aging.* New York: Springer-Verlag.

Santayana, G. (1954 [1905–1906]). *The life of reason. Volume 1: Reason and common sense.* New York: Scribner.

Schaie, K. W. (1979). The primary mental abilities in adulthood: An exploration in the development of psychometric intelligence. In P. B. Baltes & O. G. Brim, Jr. (Eds.), *Life-span development and behavior,* Vol. 2 (pp. 67–115). New York: Academic Press.

Schaie, K. W. (Ed.). (1983). *Longitudinal studies of adult psychological development.* New York: The Guilford Press.

Schaie, K. W. (1983a). What can we learn from the longitudinal study of adult psychological development? In K. W. Schaie (Ed.), *Longitudinal studies of adult psychological development.* New York: The Guilford Press.

Schaie, K. W. (1983b). The Seattle longitudinal study: A 21-year exploration of psychometric intelligence in adulthood. In K. W. Schaie (Ed.), *Longitudinal studies of adult psychological development.* New York: The Guilford Press.

Schaie, K. W. & Willis, S. (1986). Can decline in adult intellectual functioning be reversed? *Developmental Psychology 2,* 223–232.

Schaie, K. W. & Schooler, C. (Eds.). (1989). *Social structure and aging: Psychological processes.* Hillsdale, NJ: Lawrence Erlbaum.

Schatzman, L. & Strauss, A. (1955). Social class and modes of communication. *American Journal of Sociology 60,* 329–338.

Scheler, M. (1960). *Die wissensformen und die gesellschaft* (2nd ed.). Bern: Francke.

Schoenfeld, A. H. (1985). *Mathematical problem solving.* New York: Academic Press.

Schooler, C. (1972). Social antecedents of adult psychological functioning. *American Journal of Sociology 78,* 299–322.

Schooler, C. (1984). Psychological effects of complex environments during the life span: A review and theory. *Intelligence 8,* 259–281.

Schooler, C. (1987). Cognitive effects of complex environments during the life span: A review and theory. In C. Schooler & K. W. Schaie (Eds.), *Cognitive functioning and social structure over the life course* (pp. 24–49). Norwood, NJ: Ablex.

Schooler, C. (1989). Social structural effects and experimental situations: Mutual lessons of cognitive and social science. In K. W. Schaie & C. Schooler (Eds.), *Social structure and aging: Psychological processes* (pp. 129–147). Hillsdale, NJ: Lawrence Erlbaum.

Schooler, C. & Schaie, K. W. (Eds.). (1987). *Cognitive functioning and social structure over the life course.* Norwood, NJ: Ablex.

Schrader, W. B. (1965). Review of the Miller analogies test. In O. W. Buros (Ed.), *The sixth mental measurements yearbook.* Highland Park, NJ: Gryphon Press.

Sears, D. O. (1987). Implications of the life-span approach for research on attitudes and social cognition. In R. P. Abeles (Ed.), *Life-span perspectives and social psychology* (pp. 17–60). Hillsdale, NJ: Lawrence Erlbaum Associates.

Seginer, R. (1983). Parents' educational expectations and children's academic achievements: A literature review. *Merrill-Palmer Quarterly 29,* 1–23.

Shakespeare, W. (1977). *As you like it.* Ed., R. Knowles. New York: Modern Language Association of America.

Shils, E. (1983). *The academic ethic.* Chicago: University of Chicago Press.

Siegler, I. C. (1983). Psychological aspects of the Duke longitudinal studies. In K. W. Schaie (Ed.), *Longitudinal studies of adult psychological development.* New York: The Guilford Press.

Siller, J. (1957). Socioeconomic status and conceptual thinking. *Journal of Abnormal and Social Psychology 55,* 365–371.

Simmel, G. (1955). *The web of group-affiliations* (R. Bendix, Trans.) New York: The Free Press.

Simon, H. A. (1979). Information processing models of cognition. *Annual Review of Psychology 30,* 368–396.

Smith, R. B. (1985). Business and the liberal arts. *Michigan Today 17*(4): 4.

Spaeth, J. L. (1976). Cognitive complexity: A dimension underlying the socio-economic achievement process. In W. H. Sewell, R. M. Hauser, & D. L. Featherman (Eds.), *Schooling and Achievement in American Society* (pp. 103–131). New York: Academic Press.

Sternberg, R. J. (1977). *Intelligence, information processing, and analogical reasoning: The componential analysis of human abilities.* Hillsdale, NJ: Lawrence Erlbaum.

Sternberg, R. J. (1984). What should intelligence tests test? Implications of a triarchic theory of intelligence for intelligence testing. *Educational Researcher 13,* 5–15.

Sternberg, R. J. (1985). *Beyond IQ. A triarchic theory of human intelligence.* Cambridge: Cambridge University Press.

Sternberg, R. J. (1986). *Intelligence applied. Understanding and increasing your intellectual skills.* San Diego: Harcourt Brace Javanovich.

Stillings, N. A., Feinstein, M. H., Garfield, J. L., Rissland, E. L., Rosenbaum, D. A., Weisler, S. E., & Baker-Ward, L. (1987). *Cognitive science. An introduction.* Cambridge, MA: The MIT Press.

Stokes, J. P. & Levin, I. (1986). Gender differences in predicting loneliness from social network characteristics. *Journal of Personality and Social Psychology 5,* 1069–1074.

Sumner, W. G. (1906). *Folkways.* Boston: Ginn.

Tajfel, H. (1969). Cognitive aspects of prejudice. *Journal of Social Issues 25,* 79–97.

Terman, L. M. (1906). Genius and stupidity. A study of some of the intellectual processes of seven 'bright' and seven 'stupid' boys. *Pedagogical Seminary 13,* 307–373.

Thorndike, R., Hagen, E., & Sattler, J. (1986). *Guide for administering and scoring the fourth edition of the Stanford-Binet intelligence scale. Chicago:* The Riverside Publishing Co.

Van, J. (1989, February 24). Report by the American Association for the Advancement of Science on science education. *Chicago Tribune,* p. 1.

Webster's New International Dictionary, Unabridged (2nd ed.). (1960). Springfield, MA: G. & C. Merriam Publishing Co.

Wechsler, D. (1974). *Manual for the Wechsler intelligence scale for children-revised.* San Antonio, TX: The Psychological Corporation.

Wechsler, D. (1981). *Wechsler adult intelligence scale-revised manual.* San Antonio, TX: The Psychological Corporation.

Weinshank, A. B. (1985). Review of the Croft readiness assessment in comprehension kit. In J. V. Mitchell (Ed.), *The ninth mental measurements yearbook.* Lincoln, NB: Buros Institute of Mental Measurement of the University of Nebraska.

Wheeler, L., Reis, H., & Nezlek, J. (1983). Loneliness, social interaction, and sex roles. *Journal of Personality and Social Psychology 45,* 943–953.

Whitehead, A. N. (1948 [1925]). *Science and the modern world.* New York: Mentor Books.

Willingham, W. W. (1965). Review of the Miller analogies test. In O. W. Buros (Ed.), *The sixth mental measurements yearbook.* Highland Park, NJ: Gryphon Press.

Willis, S. L. & Schaie, K. W. (1986). Training the elderly on the ability factors of spatial orientation and inductive reasoning. *Psychology and Aging 3,* 239–247.

Wilson, E. O. (1980). *Sociobiology.* Cambridge, MA: The Belknap Press of Harvard University Press.

Witkin, H. A., Dyk, R. B., Faterson, H. F., Goodenough, D. R., & Karp, S. A. (1962). *Psychological differentiation. Studies of development.* New York: John Wiley & Sons.

Wuthnow, R. (1987). *Meaning and moral order. Explorations in cultural analysis.* Berkeley: University of California Press.

Zelditch, M. (1955). Role differentiation in the nuclear family. In T. Parsons & R. Bales (Eds.), *Family socialization and interaction patterns.* Reprinted in abridged form in W. Gamson and A. Modigliani (Eds.) (1979). *Conceptions of social life: A text reader for social psychology.* Washington, DC: University Press of America.

Author Index

Subject Index